HBR Guide to
Performance Management

Harvard Business Review Guides

Arm yourself with the advice you need to succeed on the job, from the most trusted brand in business. Packed with how-to essentials from leading experts, the HBR Guides provide smart answers to your most pressing work challenges.

The titles include:

HBR Guide to Being More Productive

HBR Guide to Better Business Writing

HBR Guide to Building Your Business Case

HBR Guide to Buying a Small Business

HBR Guide to Coaching Employees

HBR Guide to Data Analytics Basics for Managers

HBR Guide to Dealing with Conflict

HBR Guide to Delivering Effective Feedback

HBR Guide to Emotional Intelligence

HBR Guide to Finance Basics for Managers

HBR Guide to Getting the Right Work Done

HBR Guide to Giving Effective Feedback

HBR Guide to Leading Teams

HBR Guide to Making Every Meeting Matter

HBR Guide to Managing Up and Across

HBR Guide to Negotiating

HBR Guide to Office Politics

HBR Guide to Performance Management

HBR Guide to Persuasive Presentations

HBR Guide to Project Management

HBR Guide to
Performance Management

HARVARD BUSINESS REVIEW PRESS

Boston, Massachusetts

Copyright 2017 Harvard Business School Publishing Corporation

The web addresses referenced in this book were live and correct at the time of the book's publication but may be subject to change.

Cataloging-in-Publication data is forthcoming.

ISBN: 978-1-63369-554-2
eISBN: 978-1-63369-279-4

What You'll Learn

As a manager, you're accountable for ensuring your employees produce results that align with your organization's needs. But traditional approaches to tracking employee performance—while providing a dedicated opportunity for employee feedback and evaluation—are increasingly coming under fire. Holding a performance discussion once a year takes a lot of time and can cause stress for you and your employees—and it doesn't guarantee improvement. Organizations that use traditional performance management to engage, motivate, and develop their people are finding that those approaches don't achieve what they're after. And annual cycles that start with goal setting and culminate with a formal review aren't providing the agility you need from your employees in today's fast-paced business environment.

What you need is an ongoing, more flexible approach —one that keeps the best of the traditional performance management process but also incorporates new thinking and ideas. By following the advice in this guide, you'll discover new ways to fold managing performance into your day-to-day work, so you're monitoring employee progress, providing feedback, and offering opportunities for growth on a regular basis while still meeting any annual requirements your organization may have.

You'll learn how to:

- Help your employees set flexible goals that can adapt with the organization

- Define clear performance metrics and behavioral expectations

- Provide ongoing feedback to stop performance problems in their tracks

- Coach your people toward improvement

- Motivate your employees through recognition and rewards

- Identify growth opportunities that align with individual learning styles and preferences

- Consider development options outside the traditional promotional track

- Understand where formal appraisals are useful— and where they fall short

- Go beyond a simple number when using performance ratings

- Sidestep burnout on your team

- Manage the performance of employees who work remotely

Contents

Contents

Introduction

Performance Management for a New Age of Work

As a manager, you're responsible for the output and productivity of your team. But what steps should you take to track performance, communicate effectively with your direct reports, and encourage individual growth?

Performance management is an interconnected set of tools used to measure and improve the effectiveness of people in the workplace. High-performing organizations use performance management to achieve three goals: to develop individuals' skills and capabilities, to reward all employees equitably, and to drive overall organizational performance. As a manager, you can customize your performance management process to help your team and employees deliver strong results for the organization while helping them develop their professional aspirations.

Specific approaches to performance management differ based on organizations' strategies, values, and culture, but they typically include setting employee goals and tracking progress against these objectives, providing ongoing feedback and coaching, developing employees' skills and strengths, and, often, formal evaluations. Many elements of the process—assessing performance, giving feedback, and development, for example—are ongoing. Other activities, like goal setting and formal reviews, have historically been calendar driven and cyclical.

But traditional performance management approaches have come under fire in recent years. Many business leaders have begun to question the value of standard processes and whether they are effective in achieving the results they seek. With the growth of knowledge work, the traditional annual performance review cycle can seem like a rusty artifact ill-suited for today's nimble organizations. But stepping away from performance management entirely—leaving employees without a process for meeting their goals and managers without a method for developing their employees—risks many errors, missteps, and missed opportunities for growth. Some organizations have begun to adjust and revise their performance management processes, but even then, many managers are left wondering how to ensure the results and growth of their direct reports as more and more pieces of the process are debated.

As formal approaches to performance management evolve, managers must understand which elements of traditional best practices they should keep in place and which are fraught, which components of new processes are working and which should be avoided. This guide will introduce the essential elements of performance management so you can adjust your own process to best suit the needs of your company and your team, while also providing you with the information you need to understand the conversations surrounding performance management as it shifts to meet the needs of a changing, more agile organization.

The Evolution of Performance Management

The traditional process of managing performance began as a system for assessing and maximizing the productivity of industrial workers in manufacturing firms. The cycle generally began with the development of annual goals for each employee; at the end of the year, people were formally appraised based on how successfully they achieved those objectives. Performance assessment was based on straightforward, production-based metrics, so evaluating employees against goals was usually clear-cut: Did they produce the targeted number of units, with few errors? Appraisals were usually linked to employee ratings, which were used to calculate changes in compensation for high-performing workers. Those rated as low performing were often let go.

But processes originally developed to evaluate the performance of individual contributors in industrial firms and jobs in production don't necessarily align with the needs of today's businesses that prize creativity and innovation and those that are increasingly staffed by knowledge workers and teams whose results aren't so easy to measure. While the industrial model aimed to reduce variation (in manufacturing errors, for example), many organizations today aspire to innovate by *increasing* variation. An individual's appraisal, rating, and compensation once rested on the completion of annual goals—but today, those targets often become outdated before the year is out. In response, some organizations are embracing flexibility and shorter-term goals that can be modified over the course of the year.

Metrics to gauge performance, too, have become more complex: When an employee is dealing with ideas and knowledge rather than easily countable units, assessing performance against goals requires some ingenuity. What's more, with talent in shorter supply (and skills, particularly technical ones, becoming obsolete quickly), companies have used these metrics solely as a tool to identify individuals to advance or reward—but their actions didn't always result in better performance.

Many organizations now recognize that they need performance management processes that are better suited for their people and their needs. They want nimble, flexible instruments that can truly increase and accurately measure performance. Some organizations are shifting away from cyclical, calendar-based approaches toward those based on more communication throughout the year. Netflix, for example, eliminated formal evaluations in favor of regular performance discussions and informal 360-degree reviews, where people identify what their colleagues should stop, start, or continue doing either by supplying signed feedback or even taking part in face-to-face team meetings. Others are holding more-frequent reviews (often semiannually or quarterly) and complementing them with increased dialogue between bosses and employees that involve ongoing check-ins and opportunities for real-time feedback.

Some influential companies and business leaders are reappraising the established performance management approach—in some cases overhauling familiar processes in innovative, even unprecedented, ways. Deloitte, for example, conducted a public survey and found that 58% of executives questioned felt that their current method of managing performance neither drove employee engagement nor promoted high performance.[1] By focusing too much on looking at past results, the process provided no practical look to the future. With that in mind, Deloitte created a new approach that removed traditional elements such as 360-degree feedback, cascading objectives, and once-a-year reviews and instead focused on "performance snapshots," in which an employee's immediate manager answers four future-focused questions about an employee—essentially asking what they'd *do* with the employee rather than what they think of the individual.[2]

Companies are also discovering that a more individualized plan may work better for their employees. A different approach may be needed for, say, salaried professional staff eligible for incentive pay than for hourly employees. Some organizations are also taking steps to broaden traditional processes to weigh how teammates' contributions, in addition to system or organizational challenges, can significantly influence individual performance.

These organizations are signaling that while traditional approaches may be less effective than they once were, managers are still responsible for assessing their teams' work and output in one form or another. Few can realistically afford to dismiss the process altogether—nor should they.

Why Performance Management (Still) Matters

Despite the arguments against it, routinizing the management of employee performance can help every organization and every manager make the most of its most important resources—its people—so everyone benefits. That's because:

- Shareholders and investors observe better results when people are working in unison toward key goals.

- Supervisors are more successful when their reports focus on the right tasks and projects—and do them well.

- Employees appreciate focused goals, opportunities for career development, and recognition for outstanding performance.

An effective performance management process—one that takes into account how organizations are changing —can still keep employees focused on meaningful goals and offers managers a clear framework for appraising the quality of their people's work. At the very least, a calendar-based system—whether annual or more frequent—guarantees that direct reports will have a chance to discuss their work and get feedback from their managers at predictable intervals during the course of the year. (Managers can and should offer feedback more frequently than that, but this is a start.) The performance management cycle provides a logical time frame and process for assessing the quality of employees' work and making compensation-related decisions, whether or not companies stick with formal rating processes. And a thoughtful performance management approach will offer people opportunities to plan out learning and development efforts to boost their motivation and career satisfaction for the long term.

It's rare that an organization (or individual, for that matter) can make real progress without setting and working toward goals. And few companies can remain competitive or retain their best people without offering opportunities to grow. So as performance management evolves, it's important for managers to learn how to work within those changing processes to ensure the growth of their people and their contribution to their organization.

What's Ahead

This guide will offer tools and best practices you can tailor to manage your team's performance while meeting your organization's needs and supporting your people in today's agile business world. Whether you're looking to improve on a traditional process, seeking a more flexible option, or creating an approach where none exists, you'll learn the basics of performance management, so you can customize an approach that works for you.

In section 1, we'll explore employee goal setting: the characteristics of effective goals, how individual and organizational goals align, and how to develop metrics to measure people's progress toward their objectives. We'll also discuss creating specific plans for enabling direct reports to meet those targets to ensure that you'll be satisfied with progress. But because established goals may no longer remain static over the course of a year, we'll also explain how to assess whether set goals are still valid—and how to make changes as necessary.

In section 2, we'll discuss the process of observing, documenting, and improving performance throughout the year. You'll learn how to identify performance gaps and assess why they occur, effectively coach and deliver feedback, recognize good work, and motivate people to do their best.

In section 3, we'll address employee career development: how to ensure that your people are growing professionally. Regardless of how your organization's formal performance management process is run, employee development efforts are becoming a focus of every manager who wants to lead an engaged, high-performing team and drive business. You'll learn how to discover your employees' unique needs and ambitions, identify the tactics available to your direct reports to build their skills, determine a direction for growth, and create individualized development plans to propel people forward—even those who are struggling.

In section 4, we'll delve into the details of formal performance reviews. This section first presents current arguments for and against formal appraisals—and for those who do conduct them, offers a detailed process for success. We'll help you navigate the practice of assessing a direct report's progress toward previously established goals and show you how to put your appraisal in writing, including how to use ratings most effectively. We'll cover how to conduct the review session, from detailing performance to preparing for the review period ahead.

In section 5, we'll explore topics that managers struggle with in performance management. We'll begin by explaining how to support and nurture your B players: those who are neither ambitious standouts nor strugglers. We'll also discuss how to avoid burnout on your team—a problem that tends to affect the most valuable, hardest-working employees. Finally, you'll learn how to manage the performance of remote employees you rarely (or never) see in person.

While the rules of performance management are constantly changing, the need to work effectively with your employees and to encourage their success remains constant. This book will help you better understand how the landscape is changing, so you can adjust your own behavior while managing your people's performance and meet the needs of your organization. By following the advice in this guide, you'll be able to master each part of the process and make it an ongoing, flexible, and effective part of your daily work.

NOTES

1. Deloitte Consulting LLP and Bersin by Deloitte, "Global Human Capital Trends 2014: Engaging the 21st-Century Workforce," Deloitte University Press, 2014.

2. Marcus Buckingham and Ashley Goodall, "Reinventing Performance Management," *Harvard Business Review*, April 2015 (product #R1504B).

SECTION ONE

Goal Setting

CHAPTER 1

The Characteristics of Effective Goals

Setting clear goals is the starting point of managing performance. Goals define the results that your people should aim to achieve in a given period of time. When you work with your employees to establish targets, you help ensure that their time and energy will be spent on the things that matter most to them—and to your organization. Doing so enhances motivation, provides accountability, and boosts performance.

Agreeing on specific targets is only part of the goal-setting process, however. You must also define how your employee's progress toward these objectives will be evaluated and how to measure results and gauge behavioral expectations. Defining this information at the outset will make assessing performance easier for you later, and your employees will have a clear understanding of how to proceed throughout the year.

You will work with your people directly to craft a set of goals that are suitable for them. Before jumping into a goal-setting discussion, though, you need to know what characteristics goals should have and where to draw potential targets from. Finally, you must understand how challenging to make these objectives.

Attributes of Well-Defined Goals

Most managers are familiar with the SMART acronym, a set of five criteria that goals should meet: They should be specific, measurable, attainable, realistic, and time-bound. These five traits can be used to assess whether a goal statement has been constructed properly—like a spell-checker that can flag any misspelled words. But simply passing a SMART test isn't enough to make an objective valuable to your company or employees. A goal can be SMART without being important, challenging, or congruent with unit or organizational strategy.

Instead, consider different criteria. Effective goals must be:

- **Aligned with organizational strategy and beneficial to the company.** They focus your people's time, energy, and resources on the work that matters most.

- **Specific and measurable.** Spelling out the details of what your employee plans to achieve ensures that both of you will know when they have reached their goal.

- **Framed in time, with clear deadlines.** Including a target date for reaching a goal increases the likelihood that your employee will meet it.

- **Achievable but challenging.** Stretch goals that require individuals to reach can be energizing.

- **Future focused.** They should be geared toward improving current performance and spurring future growth.

- **Tailored to the individual.** When people are involved in setting objectives, they feel a valuable sense of ownership—and they'll naturally be more committed to things they own.

- **Documented but not forgotten.** Most organizations require that each employee's targets be written down, but too often, once they're filed away, they can fall off the radar till the next goal-setting meeting. Keeping these objectives front of mind and regularly assessing progress will prevent them from getting buried in day-to-day work.

These characteristics will help ensure that your direct reports focus their time and resources on the results that will most benefit the organization while still providing room for individual growth. Some of the attributes in this list align with SMART criteria, but you'll also see additional traits that point to a larger purpose. As you think about your employees' goals, strive to meet all of these criteria.

Sources of Goals

Each of your direct reports should have a set of goals that is based on their role, skill level, and development aims. Do this by drawing from a variety of sources directly related to your employee's needs, such as:

- **Organization, division, or department plans and strategies.** How could the employee contribute to bigger priorities? Consider your company's broader objectives, team aims, or your own targets as a manager in the process of developing an individual's goals.

- **Goals from previous review periods or those that are linked to critical job responsibilities.** Some objectives will be evergreen, and others will evolve: A salesperson will always have the goal of increasing sales, but specific numerical targets will change from year to year.

- **Comments from previous performance reviews and feedback discussions.** Perhaps there are performance gaps to close, strong skills to develop further, or greater responsibilities to take on once skills have been mastered. Performance management is a continuous process, so it can be helpful to link one period's goals with those of the next, especially when they are tied to an employee's ongoing growth or improvement.

You can also consider the "cheaper, faster, better" rubric, described by performance management expert Dick Grote in his book *How to Be Good at Performance Appraisals*. Start by thinking about the areas of an individual's job where they spend most of their time or that make the biggest impact. How can expenses be reduced (cheaper) or less time spent (faster) while still improving quality (better)? How can an employee's time and energy best be redirected to contribute to departmental or organizational success? These questions may be more apt for those with entry-level or support roles than for those in leadership positions; seeking ways to perform cheaper, faster, and better may already be a routine part of these higher-level jobs and unnecessary to identify as an additional goal.

You may be tempted to draw goals from a person's job description. After all, a well-written job description can be a clear way to define a position and its essential functions. But job descriptions tend to be more about the content of the role than about the aims that managers and their employees agree to pursue.

For example, consider this job description for an executive assistant:

The executive assistant to the director will plan, schedule, and coordinate meetings; record and circulate meeting minutes; manage and track communications by providing timely responses and distributing messages; assist in drafting, editing, copying, and distributing project reports and other materials; handle travel arrangements; assist with expense documentation and reimbursements; manage complicated schedules and day-to-day office systems; and perform other job-related duties as required.

There are many activities listed here, but not a single identifiable goal. The description doesn't provide any clarity on the objectives of the director or the organization—or about the professional ambitions of the employee. Using this write-up alone to establish effective targets for this role would be ill-advised.

As you think about potential goals for your employee (and they do the same), dig deeper than a simple job description. Think about the difference between "handle customer complaints" and "reduce customer attrition by 10%." Or "participate in a quality-control training program" versus "Cut production waste by 20%." The first is an activity, while the second is an end result to work toward. Aim toward descriptive, measurable targets in your goal setting.

The Tricky Balance of Challenge

Possibly the toughest factor in goal setting is how to make desired outcomes achievable but challenging. Stretch goals are objectives that require extra effort to reach. They're an important element of a high-performing culture and of employee development. People respond positively to challenge, and when motivated to reach a tough target, employees can push themselves to achieve more than they previously thought they could. Ambitious goals can create energy and momentum, spurring the greatest effort and highest performance. Conversely, aiming too low can lead to mediocrity. When people choose goals that are too easily attained, they don't see a need to push themselves, and they may disengage from their work.

Because they require significant effort, there's no guarantee these objectives will be achieved. And when they're too unrealistic, stretch goals can backfire. Employees may discount outcomes that are unreasonably ambitious. Faced with an impossible task or an overly aggressive objective, your direct report may end up frustrated, unmotivated, or demoralized. Worse, when faced with unrealistic targets, employees may act immorally. Michael E. Raynor and Derek Pankratz of Deloitte Consulting and Deloitte Services, respectively, have written that when trying to reach unrealistic goals, "people may feel increasingly tempted to cut corners or to resort to unethical or illegal behaviors that they would otherwise be loath even to contemplate."[1] That's not to say that all people faced with tough targets will cheat or misrepresent their performance. But driving to meet unachievable goals can pressure your employees in dangerous ways. You want your people to stretch, not to break.

Keep in mind, though, that what's an impossible ordeal for one person may be an exciting test for another. Ask an aspiring executive to lead a new team, and they may light up with excitement; ask a stellar solo contributor who had no interest in management to do the same, and you'll likely be disappointed with the results.

When developing a plan for your direct reports, collaborate with your employees to craft goals that are challenging, strategic, and in line with individual skill sets and aspirations. The next two chapters will give you the skills you need to do this.

NOTE

1. Michael E. Raynor and Derek Pankratz, "A Way to Know If Your Corporate Goals Are Too Aggressive," HBR.org, July 13, 2015 (product #H0278K).

CHAPTER 2

Define Employee Goals—and Decide How They're Measured

As a manager, you'll take the lead on setting objectives for your team as a whole. Each team member will be working toward these overarching targets, but each individual should also have unique, personalized expectations of their own.

From a purely logical perspective, goal setting should be a top-down process that begins in company strategy and cascades down from the top ranks of the organization—from the president to the VPs to the directors, all the way down the line. This system helps ensure that the goals of any employee in an organization would support their manager's team goals as well as the organization's broader objectives.

But the traditional "cascading goal" model has its downsides. When no one is able to set their own goals until their supervisor's goals have been established—which can't happen until *their* manager's goals are set—employees can feel like mere cogs in a wheel. The cascading model can directly or indirectly signal to your reports that they are truly subordinate, leaving them feeling less motivated than those who have had more ownership and control in setting their own goals. Imposed objectives dictated from on high are unlikely to motivate people as much as goals they had some say in developing. Inflexible, top-down goals can also fail to account for or take advantage of the unique interests, skills, and potential contributions of individuals throughout the organization.

Given this, consider a different approach: Let your direct reports take the lead in setting their goals. Targets that are defined by employees themselves (with managerial guidance and review) engender an important sense of ownership. A person who isn't invested in the creation of their goals may not have the same level of commitment to achieve them—and a person who isn't held accountable for results has no reason to take goals seriously. In his HBR.org article, "The Right Way to Hold People Accountable," leadership advisor Peter Bregman explains, "Accountability is not simply taking the blame when something goes wrong. . . . Accountability is about delivering on a commitment. It's responsibility to an outcome, not just a set of tasks. It's taking initiative with thoughtful, strategic follow-through."

Giving your employees the autonomy to define the details of their goals will help them take responsibility and accountability for the results they aim to achieve. It also helps ensure that they understand both the specifics and the greater importance of their objectives.

You can support your people by helping them understand what the organization's larger goals and strategy are and what your team needs to achieve. By reviewing and providing input on each objective your direct report suggests, you can help create opportunities that also support each person's growth and enable their engagement.

Set Up a Performance-Planning Session

In many organizations, new goals are set after a formal performance review, which serves as the natural end of a traditional performance management cycle and the beginning of a new one. Many experts suggest separating the review meeting from the goal-setting process for a more-focused discussion. Since appraisal sessions can cover a wide range of topics from criticism to compensation—and because many review conversations are at least somewhat emotionally loaded—separating out the goal-setting process allows you and your employee to give the conversation due consideration and focused attention. If possible, schedule a separate performance-planning session to discuss the employee's goals and your expectations.

While your employee may be setting goals for the year in this meeting, it's possible that those targets will need to be adjusted before the review period ends. In fast-changing industries, the goals you set may not be relevant for an entire year—or even for a quarter. Between constantly evolving technology and a rapidly changing economy, many organizations are becoming more agile; in that context, planning employee goals and tasks a year in advance may not be realistic or accurate. Some companies have replaced annual objectives with short-term ones. At the retailer Gap, for example, employees have quarterly targets; at GE, shorter-term "priorities" have taken the place of annual goals. Recognize that a person's goals may need to be adjusted or adapted during the year. It doesn't make sense for anyone to keep working toward an outdated target, so while you should aim to establish long-term objectives, recognize that you may need to meet again to revise or adapt them.

Before you and your employee get together at the performance-planning meeting, ask them to draft a list of goals for the two of you to review together. Give them some pointers about what makes for an effective goal, and review some promising sources for coming up with possibilities. Employees at every level should be able to articulate how their work feeds into the big-picture organizational strategy in addition to fitting with their individual strengths, skills, and ambitions.

Define Goals

When your employee has a list in place, assess their suggested goals. How do they fit into the larger picture? Can you see clear links between their expected contributions and the results they need to achieve as members of your team? Are the objectives realistic and challenging? Do they cover all the elements of the SMART rubric and meet the characteristics of well-defined goals? When reviewing the list, make sure both organizational needs and the employee's professional aspirations are accounted for.

Aligning goals with those of the organization

Each unit, team, and individual should have goals that directly support the organization's larger strategic objectives. Such alignment focuses each person's energy on the work that matters most to the company. Your employee may already understand your team and organization's strategic efforts, but don't assume that they do. Take the time now to discuss those efforts in detail. Understanding *why* a goal is important, on both an individual and an organizational level, will make it more meaningful to your employee.

With these aims in mind, review the employee's suggested list. Do each of their proposed goals line up with these big-picture efforts? Do they fit within a larger organizational or team strategy? By defining together how their goals can contribute to a larger organizational purpose, their sense of ownership and engagement can grow, and you can begin identifying which of their suggested goals should take priority.

If a target doesn't match a team or organizational aim, assess whether it's the right fit. You may be able to revise it to better serve the team or company, or you may choose to remove it from the list altogether. Also, discuss whether there are any goals that are missing from their list that would be important to add from an organizational perspective.

Aligning personal interests with professional goals

Understanding your direct reports at a personal level will help you not only in the goal-setting process but with every facet of performance management. How can the unit goals be crafted to inspire the highest level of enthusiasm and engagement from each person? What are your employees' career ambitions? Are their professional goals compatible with those the unit or organization must pursue?

By understanding your employees as individuals and learning about their personal strengths and interests, you may be able to help incorporate those elements into their professional goals. Activities that contribute to organizational success can also spur individual employee development—and people can find the intersection of professional goals and personal interests highly motivating.

Ask your team members if they would be comfortable telling you about their personal interests during your performance-planning meeting if their drafted list of goals doesn't seem to include them. Consider what adjustments can be made to workplace objectives to include those interests. A software developer with a stand-up comedy hobby may not have much opportunity to entertain at work, but if you know they thrive in the spotlight you can suggest them for any speaking opportunities that arise. A goal of delivering departmental presentations or pitching new clients may well suit their interests and skills.

WHEN PERSONAL AND UNIT GOALS CONFLICT

Every so often you'll encounter an employee who doesn't think that a unit goal is very important—at least not to them. For example, sales manager Natasha learns that Cory, her team's newest field sales representative, has a professional goal of landing a job in market research. He's in his current job only to help him gain essential skills to put on his résumé. Natasha needs to have a conversation with Cory in which she explains that, while he may want to be in a new role in the future, he has a job to do and goals to achieve in his current position. She should tell him that by achieving or exceeding his present goals, he may get the opportunity to develop skills that are applicable to market research or gain exposure to the work done by colleagues in that field.

If Cory devotes himself to meeting his sales goals and achieves strong results, Natasha will be more likely to help him get experience in his field of interest. But if he's just not willing to get on board with his team's goals, he may not be a good fit for the team or the organization.

Even employees who share identical titles and roles can adjust certain goals or take on specific tasks that best suit their interests, tap into their strengths, and reflect their personal traits. Your team of three marketers, for example, may share similar goals regarding the new marketing initiative your department is rolling out in the next few months, but each person can also have individually tailored goals that suit their unique interests. If one person likes social media, for example, they might set a goal of increasing the organization's followers and growing brand awareness on a specific platform. Their colleague with an interest in customer research and focus groups may set out to spearhead new research efforts to better target your department's marketing dollars, while another team member with a passion for data analytics could aim to analyze your current marketing effort's reach. By identifying your employee's interests, you can help them define objectives that let them explore and develop skills that are meaningful to them while producing valuable work results.

Once you've taken the time to understand your employee's strengths and aspirations, look again at their suggested list of goals to see if any align with those traits and objectives. In some cases, you may need to prioritize an organizational mission over a personal aim, but strive for balance to keep your employee engaged, motivated, and growing. (See the sidebar "When Personal and Unit Goals Conflict" for suggestions on what to do when your employees' aspirations don't match with unit goals.)

Set a Reasonable Number of Goals

Once you and your report have discussed the list of goals in detail, narrow down the list to a succinct set of objectives to pursue. Even stellar employees can only do so much. A person faced with two goals will probably make progress toward achieving both. But when faced with five, an individual may only make progress toward two or three. Any more than five, and your employee is unlikely to accomplish any, since their attention will be so divided. Instead of burying someone in a flurry of goals, prioritize: Focus on two to four challenging, specific, significant goals.

People can also be overwhelmed by complex and large goals—which is not to say they can't aim to meet them. It can be helpful, though, to break a goal into smaller pieces, or to set shorter-term aims. Setting monthly or quarterly goals, rather than annual ones, can narrow the focus enough to make the target achievable while still having a big impact.

Establish Ways to Measure Success

Once you and your employee agree on a set of meaningful goals, determine how you plan to assess progress toward each one. List anticipated outcomes and measures for each item.

Metrics provide objective evidence of goal achievement or progress toward it. Sales revenues, errors per thousand units of product, and time to market for new products are all clear examples of metrics that can be linked to goals, since they can be easily quantified.

It's worth noting, however, that not every goal can be easily measured, and you can fall into traps while establishing metrics. Keep the following pitfalls in mind as you define how objectives will be evaluated.

- **Missing metrics.** Some goals may not be obviously connected to clear performance metrics. "Increase unique visitors to the website by 5%" is simple to measure if you know the starting point, but a goal of "increase engagement on social platforms" is trickier to quantify.

- **Choosing the wrong metrics.** Not all that can be measured is equally important or worth targeting. While it's great to increase the number of customer complaints resolved in a given time period, it may be better to focus on reducing the number of complaints overall.

- **Overemphasizing metrics.** Performance is a combination of two factors: behaviors and results. If results are the "what" of performance, behaviors are the "how." Noting the behavior and work behind a specific goal is just as important as the metric itself, even if it's not easily quantifiable. Helping a colleague who's facing a tight deadline or coaching a new member of the team is unlikely to fit into anyone's formal goals, but such actions deserve recognition and acknowledgment.

When goals aren't easily quantified

Some goals are more qualitative and therefore harder to measure. In such cases, you should still be able to pinpoint tangible, measurable targets within them. If you're struggling to find a suitable unit of measure, set a more specific, metric-friendly goal targeting something that *can* be measured. Someone whose goal is to improve their public speaking skills may set a target of making six public presentations in the upcoming year, with the understanding that there will be a follow-up meeting to discuss that performance and ways to improve after each. Or, if your employee is tasked with increasing innovation, a suitable target might be to propose three new ideas to the department in the next six months or to meet certain deadlines for specific stages in a project's development.

Determine in advance how you plan to measure progress for each goal, whether it's a numerical or time-based target. Be specific: If you were evaluating an individual who wanted to improve their public speaking, you might want to agree on how you define "public presentations." Are they presentations to the department, to the organization as a whole, or outside the company? Additionally, define ways to measure engagement and people's reactions to determine if the speech was considered a success.

While goals and metrics are hugely important, they are not the be-all and end-all of performance management. Don't make the mistake of dismissing what you can't quantify. When it comes time to assess an employee's performance, you'll want to look beyond simply measured aspects.

Establish Expectations, Not Just Goals

When you discuss objectives with your employees, you should also talk about what you expect of them in terms of behavior. Your direct report may understand what they must achieve, but if they do so in a way that's detrimental to your team or the organization, their contributions won't matter.

Talk through your expectations for citizenship behaviors—like stepping in to help colleagues in need, serving as a resource for others, cooperating and demonstrating flexibility, and training new hires—as well as basic competencies like behaving professionally in the office and arriving to work on time. How individuals contribute to organizational culture may not fit into a goals framework but is still essential to achieving strong performance. Understanding behavioral expectations is important to creating a collaborative and productive work environment—and you should make it clear to your employees that you value their contributions and cooperation on this front as much as you do their work results.

When you make your expectations clear from the outset and your employees understand how they'll be evaluated, performance improves. Plus, making expectations explicit helps hold employees accountable.

CHAPTER 3

Collaborate with Your Employee to Create a Plan for Moving Forward

Once you and your employee have developed a clear set of challenging goals with specific metrics, you'll need to ensure that there's a practical plan in place for achieving them. As social psychologist Heidi Grant says, "Creating goals that teams and organizations will actually accomplish isn't just a matter of defining what needs doing; you also have to spell out the specifics of getting it done, because you can't assume that everyone involved will know how to move from concept to delivery."[1]

Goals can seem impenetrable, even overwhelming, but they become much more manageable when there's a detailed plan to reach them. An ambitious objective that will take a year to complete will be composed of many smaller parts and steps. For example, a financial services professional may set a goal of obtaining licensure for a certain specialty. It's unlikely that he'll be able to meet that goal simply by showing up for the licensure exam without any advance preparation. Instead, he'll need to break the goal down into doable components, studying for each part of the exam over a predetermined period of time.

Your employees should do the same: When people create a plan to meet a goal, they are more likely to successfully achieve it. While some such plans may be straightforward and quick to pull together, others will be more difficult to figure out. But the time you invest at the beginning of the process will pay off when your employee nimbly works through what could have been tricky steps. Remember, too, that just as goals may shift over time, plans to achieve them may need to be adjusted.

Set a Comprehensive Plan for Success

In most cases you'll want your employees to develop a plan for meeting goals that you can then review. The process of setting a plan can empower your direct report and create a sense of ownership. But in some cases, especially for challenging goals or with employees who are new to project planning, you may need to work together to complete the following steps.

Step 1: Determine the tasks needed to accomplish the goal

Break the goal down into task-based components. If one task seems overwhelming, separate it into smaller parts. Some items may be completed simultaneously (such as making tweaks to a draft marketing campaign while awaiting additional feedback), while others may need to be completed sequentially (such as getting approval for the final campaign before implementing it), so list them in the appropriate order. Determining each required task can make complex or long-term projects seem much more manageable.

Step 2: Plan the timing for each task

Set a start and finish date for each individual task, and describe the desired results or outcomes for each item. For team projects, you may be familiar with a Gantt chart or other time-scaled task diagram that illustrates an estimated schedule. A Gantt chart is an easy-to-read bar chart that clearly communicates what needs to be done in a particular time frame (see figure 3-1). The graphic shows you what tasks are upcoming and allows you to make adjustments in your plans as necessary, such as if one task takes longer than expected and subsequent ones need to be pushed forward.

Individuals can use a similar visual for their tasks by creating such a chart in an excel file or digital calendar. Mark intended milestones along the way, such as "We should have the first stage of task A completed by May 15." With your employee, create an individualized

FIGURE 3-1

Gantt chart example

Product development project

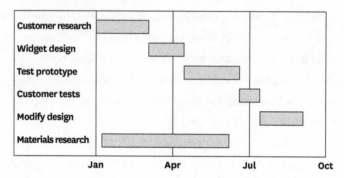

Source: *Harvard Business Essentials: Manager's Toolkit: The 13 Skills Managers Need to Succeed* (Boston: Harvard Business School Press, 2004), 11.

diagram that includes each of their tasks. Watch out for overloading or tight time crunches, where if one task moves, deadlines may be missed. This tool can then be updated throughout the review period as schedules and goals shift.

As you develop the chart, think through contingency plans. If something does move, how should your employee adapt? Discuss such possibilities with your direct report, so they can stay on track even when the unexpected happens.

Step 3: Gather the resources needed to fulfill each task

Many efforts fail because people underestimate the time and resources required to accomplish each task. Once you've planned how each task will be executed and assigned its individual time line, consider what the employee will need to complete it. Do they have the bandwidth and equipment to manage these tasks in addition to their ongoing responsibilities? Does your direct report have the training and knowledge to be successful?

In some cases you may be able to supply the additional resources your employee requires—a new piece of technology, access to a database, or colleagues to assist them. But in others, you may discover that the person needs to learn new skills, particularly if they're facing an especially challenging goal. When that's the case, discuss ways you can help your employee fill the gaps. (See chapter 9, "Expand Your Employee's Skill Sets," to read more on how to develop these proficiencies.)

Step 4: Get it on paper

Once you and an employee have reached agreement on goals and created a detailed plan to reach them, document your conclusions. Your organization may have a form you can use, or you can create your own using the template in table 3–1 at the end of this chapter. Either way, you'll want to include the following information:

- The date of your performance-planning meeting

- Key points brought up by both parties

- The employee's goals for the next review period

- A detailed plan of what is required to achieve them

- A description of any resources or training you have agreed to provide

- A time frame for follow-up meetings

Some organizations require that statements of goals be submitted to HR, but whether yours does or not, keep the document on file for yourself, and share it with your employee as well. You'll find this write-up helpful when it comes time to revise an employee's goals, for evaluating their performance throughout the review period, and in the instance of a formal appraisal.

Follow Up and Reassess Goals

Performance management is an ongoing process, so regularly schedule check-in conversations to keep track of your direct reports' progress toward both short- and long-term goals. If you don't know how well someone is doing, you won't know when to make adjustments in their plan to reach their objectives—or in the goals themselves. For example, GE encourages frequent conversations with employees to revisit two key questions: "What am I doing that I should keep doing? And what am I doing that I should change?"[2]

The timing of these check-ins can vary depending on how many employees you manage, how you work with your employees, or the general pace of your industry. In some instances your organization may have a particular recommendation. For instance, in their revamping of performance management practices, Deloitte implemented weekly check-ins. Some other companies suggest their managers check in monthly or quarterly.

You're the best judge of how frequently you should meet with each of your direct reports. At the end of your performance-planning meeting, discuss with your employee when it makes sense to check in. Some meetings should be event-based: when an employee completes a task, reaches a milestone, or achieves a goal. But others will be between these points, simply to discuss ongoing progress. Set a schedule of check-ins in advance, and put your next meeting date on the calendar before you conclude the performance-planning session. These regular conversations are the most effective and time-efficient way to stay up-to-date on your employees' performance.

When to change your employee's goals

It's possible that an employee may need to update their goals before the next performance appraisal comes around. Perhaps they've achieved a goal and need a new challenge, they're taking over responsibilities for a teammate who's shifted to a new role, or the organization's objectives have changed. For instance, the goal of developing an innovative new app may need to adjust if the organization has decided to prioritize its current mobile interface instead.

If an employee's goals need to be revised, meet to review previously set goals and plans. Three questions can guide you in your discussion as you reassess targets:

- Are they still *realistic*, given any changes in constraints or resources?

- Are they still *timely*? Is now the best possible moment to achieve them?

- Are they still *relevant*? Do they still align with the company's strategy?

It may be necessary to change only a single goal by replacing it with a new one, but in cases of major change, the entire plan may need to shift. If, for example, your team has been diligently working toward a merger, everyone will need a new set of goals after the merger happens.

If you're checking in with your direct reports on a regular basis about their progress, the need to change course or revise goals will come as no surprise. Additionally, every check-in will be another opportunity to monitor your employees' performance, offer feedback, or provide coaching. These elements of ongoing performance management are the topic of the next section.

NOTES

1. Heidi Grant, "Get Your Team to Do What It Says It's Going to Do," *Harvard Business Review*, May 2014 (product #R1405E).

2. Peter Cappelli and Anna Tavis, "The Performance Management Revolution," *Harvard Business Review*, October 2016 (product #R1610D).

TABLE 3-1

Goal-setting template

Describe the three primary goals the individual is to accomplish in the upcoming year with a description of how they will be measured and any expected outcomes.

Goals	Measures of achievement/expected outcomes
1.	
2.	
3.	

In the following section, describe specific tasks that need to be completed to accomplish each of the three goals above. Include specific time lines, plans for completion, resources needed, additional actions required for follow-up, and any contingency plans discussed.

Goal 1:

Tasks required:　　　　Start date:　　　　End date:

_____

_____

Plan to execute tasks:

Resources needed:

Actions required for follow-up:

Contingency plans:

Goal 2:

Tasks required:　　　　Start date:　　　　End date:

_____

_____

Plan to execute tasks:

Resources needed:

Actions required for follow-up:

Contingency plans:

Goal Setting

Goal 3:		
Tasks required:	Start date:	End date:

_____

_____

_____

Plan to execute tasks:

Resources needed:

Actions required for follow-up:

Contingency plans:

_____

Please include any additional notes about the
employee's goals or plan here:

_____

**This plan is agreed to as indicated by
the signatures below.**

Employee   Date

_____

Manager   Date

_____

Source: Adapted from *20-Minute Manager: Performance Reviews* (Boston: Harvard Business Review Press, 2015), 83–85.

Ongoing Performance Management

CHAPTER 4

Assessing Performance Isn't a Onetime Event

Performance management is an ongoing process, not a one-and-done event. Circumstances and priorities can shift over time, and gaps can form if employees are unable to keep up—which why so many companies are implementing more-flexible performance cycles. So it's particularly important, especially in a fast-changing work environment, that you observe the quality of your employees' performance and respond to it in the moment. In the previous section you read about defining goals and adjusting them as needed. Now we'll focus on keeping track of performance and responding to it regularly.

Unlike a time-bound formal review session (which we'll discuss in section 4), assessing performance and providing feedback is a continual process. You and your employees will both benefit if you give feedback often.

Take advantage of your check-in sessions as opportunities to track your employees' strengths, weaknesses, interests, and ambitions while also staying apprised of their progress. You'll be able to identify where your employees may be falling short of their goals and collaborate on ways to correct course.

Periodic progress checks and ongoing observation are essential in order to help you:

- **Stay grounded in goals.** Checking in to monitor progress toward goals offers the opportunity to revise targets based on changing priorities or circumstances. You might discover that your employee is on track to meet a goal ahead of schedule—or you might need to remind them about important items that may not be the current focus of their attention.

- **Recognize and reinforce strong performance.** People always welcome positive feedback about their contributions, successes, and achievements, so be liberal with your praise. In fact, some experts suggest that to boost performance, you should provide more positive feedback than negative. (To learn more about offering recognition, see chapter 7.)

- **Become aware of performance gaps, and close them.** A performance gap is the difference between someone's current performance and what is required. As a manager, it's crucial that you identify small gaps before they snowball into bigger issues.

If you're up-to-date on your direct report's progress, you'll be well positioned to catch any problems early and work with your employee to correct course—before they veer so far off target that carefully set goals become unattainable. Ongoing observation is key to staying on top of any issues and identifying the root cause of problems, as well as finding opportunities for positive feedback and recognition.

Observe and Gather Data

To best track performance, observe your employees and how they are progressing toward their goals. Your mission should be to identify an individual's strengths and weaknesses and to understand the impact that their work and behavior has on the person's ability to achieve specific objectives, as well as their contribution to the organization as a whole. You'll also want to keep ongoing notes on their performance. (See the sidebar "Document Your Observations.")

If there are periodic milestones built into your employee's goals, you'll easily be able to spot performance gaps as they develop. For example, Nadia is worried about her employee Eileen's performance. Eileen's goal is to increase sales in her territory by 10% this calendar year, but the first-quarter results show that Eileen's sales are only 2% above last year's numbers for the same period. If this trend continues, Eileen won't meet her annual goal. Nadia would be wise to check in with Eileen—earlier rather than later—to see what can be done to close the gap before it's too late.

Perhaps someone demonstrates a behavior that is causing problems. It's important to assess whether it's an anomaly that won't cause future damage or an ongoing behavior pattern that requires your immediate feedback so your employee can change. Consider these examples:

- During a team meeting, Harriet observed that her direct report Raul frequently interrupted others, preventing them from expressing their views. This tripped up team dynamics and undermined the teamwork that Harriet's unit depended on for its success.

- Miguel noticed that Leila, an off-site member of his team, often seemed the first to pipe up in brainstorming sessions with reasons why a colleague's suggestion wouldn't work. After overhearing some heated conversations between on-site teammates, Miguel became concerned that Leila's comments might be inhibiting the group.

While your own personal observations are important, in today's environment where tasks are complex or involve a team, you may not have the ability to see the full picture. It's helpful to ask for others' thoughts as well. Feedback from other sources provides a useful reality check of your own views—and may provide you with new information about additional good or bad performance. So, when appropriate, discuss these situations with trusted colleagues—in confidence. Add their observations to your own.

For example, Harriet viewed Raul's habit of interrupting others as stifling valuable dialogue, but someone else may applaud his strenuous articulation of his views. To better understand whether Raul was indeed hurting team interactions, Harriet could go to another manager, Leo, and request that he observe Raul's participation in an upcoming meeting and report back on his impressions. (Note that she should not request that the manager look for interruptions specifically, so as not to influence his thinking.) Once she hears back from Leo, Harriet will be better able to fairly assess whether Raul's interruptions are actually a hindrance to his performance. Similarly, Miguel could ask members of his team whether Leila's critiques during their brainstorming sessions are bothering others—and if so, how—to understand the impact of her actions before jumping to conclusions.

DOCUMENT YOUR OBSERVATIONS

Keep a file (electronically or on paper) on each of your direct report's performance, and update it throughout the year. Use it to keep track of both good and bad performance, so you have a balanced view of your employee's work. Update it after check-ins, or set a calendar reminder to add new information periodically.

This document will likely be only for your own reference, so you don't need to write much—just enough so you can see progress (or lack thereof) over time and ensure that you'll remember notable successes or missteps. That said, if someone's performance is suffering to the point where you need to consider termination,

(continued)

DOCUMENT YOUR OBSERVATIONS

you should be especially careful about documenting such actions, as your personal notes could become material in a legal case. Consult with your human resources department or internal legal team for guidance.

Here are a few points to consider when keeping track of performance:

- Record the date and specifics of what happened. For instance: "Raquel's pitch to a potential new client exceeded my expectations. When the client called to confirm that I'd received the signed contract, he mentioned that he and his staff were 'blown away' by her polished delivery and ability to think on her feet when answering questions."

- Stick to facts, not judgments. For example: "Larry has missed four project deadlines in the last three months" rather than "Larry doesn't know how to manage his time."

- Make notes on the day you've given someone feedback (or soon after), while it's fresh in your mind.

- Keep a folder of emails or other correspondence highlighting your employee's accomplishments, whether they are instances you noted yourself or include praise from others.

If you aren't able to check in regularly with your employees and jot down notes yourself—perhaps they work remotely or travel often—request periodic progress reports from each of them every week, month, or quarter. These reports don't need to be formal. An email with a few bullet points will suffice to gather the necessary information, such as their key accomplishments, questions or concerns, and what the individual aims to achieve before the next report or check-in session. You'll be able to gather additional information about each person's performance based on the quality and timeliness of the reports.

These informal records will help you when annual review time rolls around, but they'll also keep you in the loop on any developing performance gaps and help you identify opportunities to offer timely feedback and coaching throughout the year.

Always ensure you have a complete picture of the situation, and continue to watch your direct report's work and behavior if you have any doubts about your perceptions. Avoid premature judgment, and recognize that, no matter someone's behavior, any assumptions about the causes are just that—assumptions. Instead, consider what might underlie an employee's disappointing work results, and make the effort to accurately assess what's causing the problem.

Notice subtle requests for help

While observation is essential to understanding performance, it's also important to perceive the indirect ways your employees may be asking for help. People don't always know what kind of help they need or exactly how to ask for it. Sales manager Rita, for example, was frustrated by the vague monthly reports she was getting from Philip, a salesperson on her team. In their check-in meetings he asked few questions, but after receiving more similarly unsatisfactory reports, Rita realized that Philip might have dropped hints that he wasn't sure what information she was looking for.

Make a practice of actively listening when discussing projects or progress with your employee, and confirm that they understand exactly what you're asking of them. Some people, reluctant to show they're not clear on something, may subtly drop hints rather than ask for clarification directly. Tune in—what you hear may help you figure out how to improve a person's work.

Identify Possible Causes of Poor Performance

If you've noticed an employee's work isn't up to par, your next step is to investigate what may be causing the issue. The underlying cause could be a skill deficiency, poor time management or personal work habits, lack of motivation, conflict with another employee, or unclear direction on your part. Or it could be something else entirely, like a misunderstanding of expectations.

Underperformance may have a nonobvious cause and have nothing to do with lack of skill or motivation. Here are a few possible reasons why people may fall short of expectations:

- **Bad processes.** W. Edwards Deming, one of the great management teachers of the past century, warned business leaders that the source of unsatisfactory performance was usually bad work processes. If you want better performance, look to the work process before you look for faults in your people. Perhaps your employee who is frustratingly late in delivering documents is being hampered by a cumbersome approval process that relies on getting sign-offs from someone who travels often or doesn't always turn requests around quickly.

- **Workplace tensions.** Workload inequities (even if temporary) or simply a visceral dislike may produce conflict that impairs performance. Perhaps two teammates have both applied for a higher-level position; when one is promoted, the other may grow resentful. Another common—and easily remedied—cause of workplace tensions is communication style differences between colleagues. If you can discover what's behind conflict or tension, you may be able to neutralize it.

- **Work overload.** Even the most-committed employee will burn out if you demand too much too fast, so beware of unreasonably ambitious goals and expectations. Don't set the bar too high. If you notice after a series of check-ins that someone has yet to make progress toward a goal, ask what's holding them back; doing so may lead you to reassess the objective. Temporary situations can also affect the quality of an employee's or even a team's work. If one team member misses a number of days of work to tend to an ill family member, for example, their colleagues may feel supportive but also overburdened from picking up the slack.

- **Personal problems.** Sometimes the root cause of poor performance may have nothing to do with work at all. A health crisis at home may be distracting your direct report, or an employee may be struggling to manage both workplace and family demands. You might be able to help mitigate these problems if you learn what they are. For example, if an employee is stretched thin between caring for young children as well as aging parents, perhaps you can offer a flexible work schedule or an option to work remotely on occasion to allow the individual to aid their family.

If you notice poor performance, remember that there may be underlying issues that you need to identify before moving forward with a plan of action. Remedies will differ depending on the cause.

Are you part of the problem?

As you consider possible reasons behind a performance gap, assess whether you've played a role in the issue. Ask yourself if you've unwittingly thrown up roadblocks by, say, reducing necessary resources, overloading your employee with responsibility, or micromanaging. Consider these questions:

- **Have I been clear in my expectations?** It's possible that your employee may not know exactly what you're looking for. If you suspect a lack of clarity is the issue, ask your direct report to explain the task or project in their own words, instead of simply asking whether or not they understand you.

- **Am I holding up my end of the bargain?** Perhaps you and your employee have agreed that they need to step up their leadership skills and take on more responsibility—but when they tried to take ownership of a recent project, you insisted on daily updates. While this might not seem like an unreasonable request, to your employee, it could appear that you distrust them and are micromanaging.

- **How often and to what extent have I intervened in the employee's area of responsibility?** If their performance doesn't measure up, maybe it is because you overruled their decisions or insisted that they follow *your* approach to completing the work. Some people learn best by doing research and preparing beforehand, but others thrive with a less cautious approach. Action-oriented individuals may need more freedom to experiment in order to master new skills.

- **Have I changed priorities and assigned tasks without employee input?** Perhaps you assigned an employee a new short-term project, underestimating how much time it would take away from their longer-term goals. Or you might have given an assignment that was impossible to complete on time. An unexpected—and unplanned for—shift in time or resources can throw anyone off their game.

When you have identified the cause of a problem, decide if it's worth addressing. Is this a true performance gap or a temporary glitch? If it was a onetime misstep unlikely to be repeated—an error made the first time a person used a new tool or attempted a new task, perhaps—you might let it go. Avoid giving feedback, too, in situations where your employee can't change or control the outcome. If they're being held up by someone else's delayed sign-off, for example, then they may not be the appropriate target for your feedback. Something that you deem to be a problem may simply be a matter of preference. Harriet may find Raul's habit of interruption annoying, but if it has no effect on team dynamics or performance, it may make sense to overlook it.

On the other hand, if you discover a performance problem that could happen again if not addressed, plan to discuss the issue sooner rather than later. The next chapter will guide you through the process of delivering effective feedback.

CHAPTER 5

Make a Habit of Providing Feedback

Feedback can be a useful tool for addressing performance gaps and recognizing exemplary work. In the same way that periodic tests and assignments help both teachers and students gauge progress over the course of a semester before the final exam, ongoing feedback keeps both you and your employee on top of how they are performing as they work toward their goals. Even companies that have done away with traditional elements of the performance management process—goal setting or formal annual reviews—still rely on regular feedback. In fact, many organizations are asking managers to offer it more frequently, as it's one of the most flexible and effective tools available for getting results from your people.

Make giving feedback a regular part of your ongoing performance management approach as a way to recognize good work and redirect missteps in progress.

The Two Types of Regular Feedback

Ongoing feedback falls into one of two main categories. Positive feedback or praise—*Here's what you did really well*—can enhance confidence and increase an employee's sense of commitment. Constructive feedback—*Here's where you need to improve*—is informative, providing a basis for discussion and redirection. Whatever the type, feedback is most effective when it's grounded in specific details that an employee can use.

Positive feedback should pinpoint particular actions of merit: "I liked how you handled the prototype demonstration. The way you began with the underlying technical challenges, went on to describe how those obstacles were addressed, and finished with the actual demonstration helped us all understand the technology." While vague praise—"Great job with that prototype demonstration!"—may not do harm, it doesn't communicate much useful information.

Constructive feedback should target specific opportunities for improvement: "Your demonstration suffered from a lack of organization. I wasn't sure of the problem the prototype aimed to solve, and the technical challenges weren't well-defined." Clear statements help an employee understand what to work on. On the other hand, unvarnished criticism—"People in the audience were bored and confused by your demonstration"—is neither specific nor helpful and offers neither insight nor room for improvement.

Specific feedback, both positive and constructive, is effective at different times with different types of people. Positive feedback is especially helpful for employees at early stages of their career or for individuals who are trying to master new things. "When you don't really know what you are doing, encouragement helps you stay optimistic and feel more at ease with the challenges you are facing—something novices tend to need," social psychologist Heidi Grant explains in her HBR.org article "Sometimes Negative Feedback Is Best."

More-experienced employees, on the other hand, will likely find constructive criticism more helpful and informative, showing them where they should expend their efforts and how they might improve. "When you are an expert and you already know more or less what you are doing, it's constructive criticism that can help you do what it takes to get to the top of your game," says Grant. Seasoned professionals and high performers tend to be hungrier for and more appreciative of constructive feedback that helps them advance even further.

Frequent feedback is necessary for all your employees —even your top performers. Don't assume your top performers know how well they're doing or how much you appreciate them. "The higher the performer, the more frequently you should be providing feedback," says Jamie Harris, a senior consultant at Interaction Associates.[1] People may find constructive feedback easier to take in when they feel genuinely appreciated for what they've done well.

While providing input on an employee's work can be uncomfortable for many managers, it's important to make your feedback frequent and timely. "The primary reason people struggle with giving and receiving feed-back is not a lack of proficiency but of frequency," notes social scientist and author Joseph Grenny in his HBR.org article "How to Make Feedback Feel Normal." Check-ins provide opportunities for you to regularly assess prog-ress toward goals and discuss your direct report's perfor-mance, but don't hold off on giving feedback right away just because you have a meeting on the calendar set for a later date. Even a short debrief can be useful. For ex-ample, use the two minutes it takes to walk back to your office after a meeting to offer your employee feedback on their presentation—what they did well or how they could improve for next time. With constructive comments es-pecially, it's important to give feedback as soon as possi-ble after you've observed a behavior you want to correct or reinforce.

If you're like most managers, addressing employees about problems and pointing out their shortcomings is the least enjoyable part of your job. No one likes to de-liver bad news or tell someone that their work or behav-ior is unacceptable. But if you avoid relaying the mes-sage, the employee's unsatisfactory work or behavior will most likely continue—or worsen.

If you feel a natural reluctance to confront poor per-formance, remind yourself:

- If your aim is to improve performance, giving feedback is the most effective and efficient tool for redirecting and enhancing your employees' work.

- Not giving feedback will undermine the team. Poor performers demoralize others and thwart the success of the unit as a whole.

- You're doing that person a favor. The poor performer may actually think that they are doing satisfactory work. A frank discussion will clear up the misconception and give the employee an opportunity to improve, perhaps saving their job.

- Some employees *like* getting constructive feedback. Since it's essential to improving performance—and, by extension, to career development—many people find it valuable.

When you see an issue that needs to be addressed, don't avoid confrontation. Having an honest discussion about performance problems isn't fun for either of you, but when the conversation is over you'll know that your employee is on the right track for improvement.

Conducting the Feedback Discussion

The feedback you give will most likely cover a wide range of topics, and you'll want to tailor your delivery to the particular situation you're discussing as well as the person you're talking to. But there are some general guidelines you can follow when providing feedback.

Set the stage for a productive conversation

Before you sit down with your employee, make a few notes about what you want to say. Your goal is to elicit positive change in future performance or workplace behavior, not to rake someone over the coals for past failures, so don't dwell on the past. If your direct report

Deepa had a rocky time running her first new-employee orientation session, for example, cast your comments in the light of improving her next event. Give some thought to the most important things you can help her do better next time, rather than enumerating all the flaws you saw.

Next consider the logistics of your conversation. Be thoughtful about when you offer unexpected feedback. You don't want to risk throwing your employee off balance with constructive feedback if emotions are running high or they're due to deliver an important presentation later that day. Nor do you want to minimize the effect of giving positive feedback because you're rushing back from a meeting that ran late—or cut a productive feedback conversation short to get to your next commitment. Choose a time close enough to the event that it is fresh in everyone's minds, while still taking into account other considerations. You might, for example, wait a day (or at least a few hours) before talking to Deepa about the orientation session rather than addressing it immediately, especially if she seems flustered or frustrated. Let her cool down so that when you do deliver your message, she'll be primed to hear it.

Choose a meeting place where you won't be distracted or interrupted. You'll want to conduct the conversation in a location where you both can easily hear each other and where you're free from social interactions that could inhibit your employee from being open and honest. That doesn't necessarily mean you need to meet in your office, if you think your employee might find that intimidating. An afternoon discussion over coffee in the quiet company cafeteria could work well, but meeting in the cafeteria during a busy lunch hour won't allow either of you to devote your due attention to the conversation.

Engage in a two-way dialogue

A feedback conversation gives each party an opportunity to tell their side and to hear the same from the other. If your goal in delivering feedback is to elicit change, your best tool is a two-way discussion, not a monologue. It's easy for an employee to shut down when feeling criticized, so to make progress, involve them in the conversation. Deliver your feedback, and give your employee your undivided attention. Listen to what they have to say, but also note physical cues, such as a grimace or crossed arms. What are they expressing, verbally or otherwise? (See the sidebar "Be an Active Listener.")

Open the conversation by soliciting the person's thoughts or reactions to assess if you see the problem in a similar light. Perhaps your greatest concern about Deepa's orientation session was her delivery, but she thinks the technical issues with showing her slide deck was the main problem. Don't impose your own judgment at first. Start with an evenhanded question, such as "Deepa, how do you think the orientation session went?"

Asking the right questions will help you understand the other person and their view of performance. Open-ended and closed questions will yield different types of responses. Open-ended questions invite participation and idea sharing. Use them to get the other person talking and for the following purposes:

- **To clarify causes of a problem.** "What do you think the major issues are with this project?"

- **To uncover attitudes or needs.** "How do you feel about our progress to date?"

- **To explore alternatives and feel out solutions.** "What would happen if . . . ?"

Closed questions, by contrast, lead to yes or no answers. Ask closed questions for the following purposes:

- **To focus the response.** "Is the project on schedule?"

- **To confirm what the other person has said.** "So your main issue is scheduling your time?"

Thoughtful questioning can help you uncover the other person's views and deeper thoughts on the problem, which will help you formulate an effective response.

Stick to facts, not opinion

Move on to sharing your point of view, but focus on ob-served behaviors, not assumptions about character traits, attitudes, or personality. A specific comment that relates to the job—for example, "I've noticed that you haven't offered any suggestions at our last few brainstorming sessions"—opens the door for your employee to explain why. But an opinion-based statement, more often than not, can shut down the conversation entirely.

For example, an opinion-based statement like "You just don't seem engaged with your work" paints the person into a corner and invites a defensive, opinion-based

BE AN ACTIVE LISTENER

If your goal is to understand what is going wrong with your employee's performance, you must listen. You might miss out on important information if you carry too much of the conversation, suggest solutions before your employee does, or busy your mind with thoughts of what you'll say next. Instead, really focus on what your employee is saying.

To learn as much as possible from discussions with your employees, practice active listening, which encourages communication and puts others at ease. Try these tactics:

- *Give your employee your full attention.* Maintain eye contact and a comfortable posture.

  Allow time for the other person to gather their thoughts before chiming in to fill the silence. Don't interrupt, and avoid distractions like checking your phone.

- *Observe body language.* Do the speaker's expression and tone of voice match what's being said? If not, you might want to comment on the disconnect and ask to hear more.

- *Reflect what you see and hear.* To acknowledge the speaker's emotions—which will encourage them to express themselves further—describe what you're observing without agreeing

(*continued*)

BE AN ACTIVE LISTENER

or disagreeing. "You seem worried about . . ." Acknowledge if they seem to be struggling; this will demonstrate your empathy and make your employee feel recognized. "I can imagine you're having a hard time with . . ."

- *Paraphrase what you hear.* Check to make sure you understand what the speaker is saying. "So if I hear you right, you're having trouble with . . ." "If I understand, your idea is . . . Does that sound right?"

To give feedback effectively, you need to receive and truly hear what your employee has to say. A productive conversation, especially about a possibly sensitive performance gap, is a two-way street.

reply: "You're wrong. I *am* engaged." This isn't productive for either of you. Statements about assumed motivations can quickly lead to your employee becoming guarded, which will make it nearly impossible to persuade them to change. To make any progress, you need your employee to be a receptive, active participant in this discussion.

Instead, offer a specific observation that's free of personal judgment. To Deepa, for instance, you might say, "I noticed that you looked down at the AV equipment a lot during the orientation session and missed opportunities to see when someone had a question." This is an observation you viewed that Deepa can then respond to, rather than feeling like she needs to defend herself.

Be specific about the problem and its impact on others

Your employee may not be fully aware of the consequences of their behavior, so lay it out clearly. For example, "Deepa, because you were looking down during most of your presentation, our new hires were unable to ask the questions they had and were unsure of some of the policies you presented. I heard some frustration from the group afterward, and they may be unclear as to how to proceed when issues arise in the coming weeks." The details demonstrate that this is a real problem, not a matter of your preference, and that it impacts not only you but others as well.

Managers sometimes mistakenly think they need to act tough when giving constructive feedback. But the aim of feedback should be to motivate change, not to make your employee feel attacked. When people feel threatened, they're unlikely to really hear what you're saying, let alone absorb or apply it. Take a thoughtful, nonaggressive approach to allow the receiver to take in, reflect on, and learn from your feedback. "Deepa, let's discuss how you might modify the planning process for the next orientation session. I know this last one didn't go well, but I'm confident you can improve for next time."

It can be tempting to couch constructive feedback in praise, in an attempt to soften the blow. Sweetening your message may lessen your own anxiety about delivering bad news, but it also diminishes your employees' ability to receive it. This "sandwich" approach actually undermines your ability to communicate any meaningful feedback, either positive or constructive. Employees who are struggling may lose track of where they need to change, registering only the compliment—and high achievers may dismiss positive feedback as a mere preamble to the "real" message.

Ask how your employee can address the problem

People generally feel more ownership of solutions they suggest themselves, but if your direct report has trouble coming up with a reasonable suggestion for change, offer one yourself and check for understanding. It's important that the employee leave the conversation with a concrete step for improvement. For example, "In the future, let's arrange for you to organize practice sessions in advance of orientation meetings, so you can rehearse what you plan to say, get used to the equipment, and hear some of the questions our new hires are likely to ask." Then, check for the receiver's understanding of your suggestion: "Does this sound feasible to you?" If they seem iffy or unclear on the plan for improvement, ask them to explain it in their own words so you can assess if they've truly grasped it. If your direct report can clearly explain what they should change or do next, you've curtailed the need to deliver the same feedback again—and if the message is muddled, you can clarify it on the spot.

In some instances, you may discover that a onetime feedback discussion isn't enough to close a performance gap. In those situations, you may need to consider coaching your employee, which is the topic of the next chapter.

NOTE

1. Quoted in Amy Gallo, "Giving a High Performer Productive Feedback," HBR.org, December 3, 2009, https://hbr.org/2009/12/giving-a-high-performer-produc.

CHAPTER 6

Coach Your Employees to Close Performance Gaps

Coaching is a powerful way to encourage your employees' growth and a practical approach for developing new skills. It can also be used to close performance gaps. But coaching—an ongoing learning process in which you help your direct reports build mastery—usually won't bring about a quick fix. When you need a fast turnaround or immediate results, feedback is your best bet. When an employee is driven to improve and wants your help tackling a problem or building mastery, however, coaching is a rewarding and effective option.

Coaching is a supportive rather than a directive approach that relies on asking questions. According to executive coach Ed Batista, coaching is "asking questions that help people discover the answers that are right for them."[1] As a manager, you're often in the role of expert, providing answers and guidance. But in coaching, it's important to adopt a different mindset. Rather than suggest what your employees should do or explain how to do it, you should prompt your employees with questions to help them solve problems in new ways themselves. As Candice Frankovelgia of the Center for Creative Leadership says, "If you keep providing all the answers, people will keep lining up at your door looking for them."[2]

Since coaching is an ongoing time commitment, target your coaching to situations where you will get the highest return on your time and effort. The most-productive opportunities generally arise in these situations:

- A new employee needs direction.

- A direct report is almost ready for new responsibilities and just needs a bit more help.

- A newly minted manager under your wing is still behaving as though they were an individual contributor.

- A strong performer is eager to develop a new skill or explore career development opportunities.

- A significant performance problem has arisen in an employee's work.

As indicated in this list, coaching can be an effective way to help employees learn new skills so they can reach the next level in their career. But it can also be a powerful tool when it comes to closing performance gaps. As with feedback, the goal of coaching is not to reprimand your employees for shortfalls but to catalyze their growth and improvement. Your objective is not to simply identify what they did wrong (thereby draining motivation) but to elicit positive change. Because coaching requires that your employee be an active participant in their own development, it can have a deeper impact than outside-in sources of information.

Coaching may not be a fit for every employee—and it won't succeed unless the person is willing to do it—but it is broadly applicable and can be used with everyone from high-potential standouts to underperformers. As a manager, you set the overall direction for your employees; with coaching, you can help them figure out how best they can get where they need to be.

Get Your Employee Onboard

When you've pinpointed a coaching opportunity, talk it over with your employee to make sure they agree there is indeed a problem to fix or room for growth and that they are willing to tackle it through coaching. Agreement is the foundation of successful coaching: For it to work, the person must take ownership and responsibility of the process. If you intuit that an individual isn't invested in this approach, do some digging before expending more of your time. Do the two of you see the problem or opportunity the same way? Do they seem to *want* to improve?

If there's a disconnect, discuss how they would prefer to address the problem. It could be that they are open to coaching but would prefer to work with an outside coach rather than with you, their manager. Or perhaps they'd rather try taking a class before embarking on an intense one-on-one learning experience. On the other hand, if they are open to coaching with you, identify at the start of the process exactly what they're hoping to get out of it.

Define the Purpose of Your Coaching

Encourage your employee's participation by finding out what they hope to achieve and how they think coaching can help address the performance gap. You may want to begin by asking them to share their thoughts before you offer your own. By opening with a question, explains executive coach Amy Jen Su, "you'll begin as you hope to continue: with your employee talking, you listening, and both of you then building solutions together."[3]

Identify an explicit goal to target with coaching. This should be a separate goal from the performance goals your employee identified in section 1 and should generally be focused on learning. For instance, a coaching goal may to develop a new skill, learn a new behavior, or improve in a specific area, rather than to deliver specific work results.

Perhaps the two of you determine that your employee's performance gap can be closed or minimized by, say, improving delegating skills, running meetings, or prioritizing requests with tight deadlines. Once you nail down the purpose of your coaching, you may be tempted to fix the problem right away by sharing your hard-won wisdom, giving advice, or offering your opinion on what's going wrong. Resist that temptation. Encourage your employee to find their *own* answers. Instead of offering (unsolicited) solutions, ask questions to get more information.

Understand Your Employee's Perspective

To help your direct report, you need to learn more about their point of view on the performance gap and which skills they need to master in order to close it. Getting background information is critical in assessing the root causes of their challenge—and identifying an effective response.

Skillfully worded, open-ended questions can help draw out answers. Yes-or-no questions and those that begin with "why" can make people feel defensive. Start your questions with *what, how, when,* or *tell me more.* For example, you might ask the following of someone interested in developing their comfort around presenting to senior management:

- What was different or similar about the situations in which you were effective compared with those when you were less effective?

- How would you describe your effectiveness in presenting to this audience in the past?

- When have you been more or less successful in these types of interactions?

- Tell me more about what you think holds you back in these situations.

Listen deeply to your employee's answers. When someone senses you're completely focused and actively listening to what they say, it can be a deeply validating experience that helps build rapport and trust (see the sidebar "Building Mutual Trust").

BUILDING MUTUAL TRUST

Your people need to trust you. Otherwise, they have no reason to respect your judgment, do what you ask (especially if it's difficult), or put in the extra effort that results in high-quality work. Managers must earn—not demand—their employees' commitment. Establishing trust takes conscious effort. You can develop trust with your direct reports in a few different ways.

First, demonstrate ongoing concern for other people's well-being and success. People trust those who have their best interests in mind, so show empathy for your employees. When asking someone to work extra hours on a weekend to complete a strategic project, for example, acknowledge that it's an imposition: "This is an important initiative for the company, and I know that this may be an inconvenience. Would this upset any plans you've made with friends or family?" You can also build trust over time by demonstrating a genuine interest in an employee's career. Help them find opportunities to expand their horizons and develop skills that align with their professional aspirations.

You can also show your expertise in the matter at hand. According to Linda Hill and Kent Lineback, authors of *Being the Boss*, "You need to know not just what to do and how to do it but also how to get it done in the organization and the world where you work."[4] Ultimately, people grow to trust you through your accomplishments—the savvy decisions you make, your ability to garner necessary resources to make things happen, and your mastery of the concrete details of getting things done. For example, the person you are coaching with sales techniques will trust you if you yourself have a reputation as a successful salesperson.

Finally, be true to your word. Whenever you say, "Here's the plan: I'll do X and you'll do Y," be sure to hold up your end of the bargain—every time. This includes practicing discretion where appropriate. Don't disclose information held in confidence. Discussions with an employee about a performance problem in a feedback or coaching session may inadvertently dredge up personal information that the employee would not want shared with others. Always respect their privacy.

See the Problem in New Ways

With a stronger understanding of the situation, you can open a two-way dialogue to help your direct report consider new choices, strategies, or skills they might develop. This is different than offering a solution—instead, it leads your employee closer to developing their own answers. Try these tactics to establish a productive dialogue:

- **Hold up the mirror.** Redescribe the situation they have outlined to you, paraphrased from your own perspective, and ask for their response. For example, "Based on what you've told me, it seems that two things might be creating the issue. Do those ideas resonate?"

- **Reframe the situation.** Offering another angle can help your employee see things differently. Say, "Could I offer another perspective on the situation?"

- **Rehearse.** A coaching session is a safe environment to role-play an upcoming interaction, such as how they might interact with senior management. You can also review a presentation that they delivered well to this audience and discuss what made it effective. Or you can go over how they should prepare for these kinds of meetings and fine-tune preparation techniques.

The observations, suggestions, and practice opportunities you offer are the heart of your coaching session. To be effective, they need to be tailored to your employee's particular situation—and they likely should be complemented with ongoing "homework" that will help your direct report prepare for your next meeting.

Agree on Next Steps

Near the end of your coaching session, assess whether your employee is ready to move forward by asking them to summarize what they've learned. "What are the top two or three things you're taking away from this conversation?" Inviting them to articulate their gains, rather than doing it yourself, increases their engagement in the process and also helps you gauge what they've taken in and what they might still need to learn.

To maintain momentum between coaching sessions, set a date for when you'll meet again, and identify any tasks to be completed before then. Rather than assigning tasks, build your employee's accountability by asking them to formulate and implement their plans, and establish associated deadlines for each clearly defined action. Perhaps, for example, they'll outline a forthcoming presentation for the group that the two of you will rehearse in your next meeting.

It could be that you leave the session with homework, too. For instance, you may need to provide your employee with additional resources, like potential training programs, or introduce them to a colleague who will make a great mentor (to read more about setting your direct report up with an appropriate mentor or sponsor, see chapter 9).

Keep the Relationship Going

Coaching doesn't end after the first meeting. Effective coaching to close performance gaps and encourage growth includes checking in to track progress and ensure understanding. Doing so gives you an opportunity to prevent backsliding, reinforce learning, and continue individual improvement.

Your employee may have found it motivating to set a target date for mastering a new skill, but don't wait until then to assess how things are going. In a fast-paced workplace, it's easy to lose track of longer-term plans and agreements. Hold yourself and your employee accountable by sticking to your planned check-in dates, and follow through with the resources or introductions you agreed to provide. Your employee is more likely to take your coaching efforts seriously if you keep your commitments.

Then, observe growth and communicate impact. Over time, are you seeing progress in your employee's results, behavior, or relationships? Explicitly communicate to your direct report the impact of the progress you observe —it may be hard for them to recognize it themselves. Helping them acknowledge changes and growth can increase their motivation.

It's unrealistic to expect an employee to immediately master skills they've been without for years, so expect a few stumbles in the process. Perfection isn't necessary for someone to make real progress. Remind yourself that you may not see results right away. When you do see improvement, celebrate a direct report's successes, even if they still have room to grow.

Of course, there's no one single right way to coach employees. What works for one person may be ineffective for another. Try different approaches, and make needed adjustments. And don't expect to master the practice of coaching right away, especially if you're new to it or to management. Like any new skill, it requires practice and stepping out of your comfort zone, which can feel awkward at first.

Not every manager will choose to use coaching as a performance management tool on a regular basis, but for the right employees, it can be a rewarding experience.

NOTES

1. Ed Batista, "Introduction: Why Coach?" in *HBR Guide to Coaching Employees*, Harvard Business Review Press, 2015, xii.

2. Candice Frankovelgia, "Shift Your Thinking to Coach Effectively," *HBR Guide to Coaching Employees*, Harvard Business Review Press, 2015, 4.

3. Amy Jen Su, "Holding a Coaching Session," in *HBR Guide to Coaching Employees*, Harvard Business Review Press, 2015, 41.

4. Linda Hill and Kent Lineback, "To Build Trust, Competence Is Key," HBR.org, March 22, 2012, https://hbr.org/2012/03/to-build-trust-competence-is-k.

CHAPTER 7

How to Keep Your Employees Motivated

Motivation is at the very heart of performance manage-ment—something that managers must attend to all the time. A person can understand the importance of ambi-tious goals but is unlikely to achieve them without be-ing motivated to do so. Feedback or coaching efforts, no matter how extraordinary, will go unheeded by an em-ployee who's disinterested. Hours invested on someone's annual performance appraisal and discussion will be largely wasted if the employee doesn't feel the need to improve.

By contrast, for those who are motivated, every aspect of performance management can serve as an opportu-nity to learn and grow. How can you inspire engagement and boost motivation on your team?

Cultivate a Culture of Respect

Motivating your people starts with being a good manager. A company can offer great pay and benefits, employee-friendly policies, and other perks, but a bad boss can neutralize these features and demotivate people. By the same token, a terrific manager can redeem an employee's experience in even dysfunctional organizational cultures.

Employees value being treated with respect—and feel it's important that their colleagues are treated well, too. For the second year running, "respectful treatment of all employees at all levels" was cited as the leading contributor to employees' job satisfaction in the Society for Human Resource Management's 2016 Employee Job Satisfaction and Engagement survey.

Unfortunately, respect isn't the norm everywhere; to the contrary, incivility and bad behavior are far too common in the workplace. Unchecked rudeness, bullying, and abusive comments create an environment where people feel threatened and fearful. When such behavior comes from bosses, in particular, it can easily spread. Fear demotivates people, spurs excessive caution, and forces people to prioritize self-protection over workplace contribution.

In their research on sustainable individual and organizational performance, business and management professors Gretchen Spreitzer and Christine Porath found that motivation and performance plummet in response to offensive behavior: "[H]alf of employees who had experienced uncivil behavior at work intentionally decreased their efforts. More than a third deliberately decreased the quality of their work. Two-thirds spent a lot of time avoiding the offender, and about the same number said their performance had declined."[1] Rudeness in the workplace costs organizations dearly and is insidiously infectious. "Those who have been the targets of bad behavior are often, in turn, uncivil themselves," Spreitzer and Porath found. Such "uncivil" behaviors include sabotaging peers, spreading gossip, and neglecting to copy colleagues on communications.

Although Spreitzer and Porath's research shows the negative effects of incivility, additional research by Porath also emphasizes the benefits of a respectful culture, as figure 7-1 indicates. Engagement rises as respectful treatment increases. And there are a few steps you can

FIGURE 7-1

When leaders treat you with respect, you're more engaged

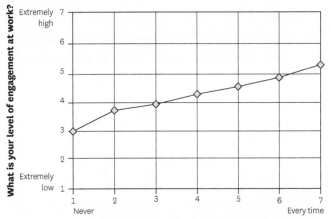

Note: Based on a study of nearly 20,000 employees around the world.

Source: Analysis of "What Is Your Quality of Life at Work?" survey data by Christine Porath. Originally published in "Half of Employees Don't Feel Respected by Their Bosses," HBR.org, November 19, 2014 (product #H012O0).

take as a manager to minimize bad behavior and foster a culture of respect, thereby boosting motivation and engagement.

- **Model good behavior.** Managers establish the tone—or lack thereof—in their workplace. A survey conducted by Porath and global leadership professor Christine Pearson found that a quarter of managers who admitted to behaving uncivilly said they did so because their own leaders and role models were rude.[2] As a manager, you have a unique opportunity to set an example of respectful treatment. Employees who see that higher-ups tolerate or embrace offensive behavior may follow suit. By contrast, when they see that a manager won't abide such behavior, they'll be less likely to engage it in themselves.

- **Respect your employee's dignity.** Discourage public criticism. A basic tenet of supervision is to praise in public and criticize in private. Being reprimanded in front of one's colleagues can have devastating effects on an employee's sense of fairness, pride, and motivation. You cannot motivate people whom you have stripped of their dignity. Some bosses inadvertently behave in ways that not only humiliate the individual target of criticism but also reduce trust among all team members who witness such incivility. Treat your employees with respect at all costs, even when you must share constructive feedback about their performance.

- **Hire respectful candidates—and stop bad behavior.** Caiman Consulting, a management consultancy headquartered in Redmond, Washington, boasts a 95% retention rate—which director Greg Long attributes to the firm's culture. In hiring, it conducts background checks, including "a candidate's record of civility." "People leave a trail," says Long. "You can save yourself from a corrosive culture by being careful and conscientious up front." Candidates who don't fit the culture, no matter how qualified, are not hired. [3]

Take note of the behavior of those already on your team. If you see a direct report being disrespectful, address it immediately. You may also want to reassure, in confidence, the recipient of that person's rudeness that you have responded to this issue. This will communicate that you're invested in the well-being of everyone on the team.

Once you've established a workplace where your employees are comfortable, you can increase their engagement through rewards, recognition, and challenge.

Truly Rewarding Rewards

"To many people, motivation and rewards go together like peaches and cream. They are inseparable," write Jeremy Hope and Steve Player in their book *Beyond Performance Management*. Rewards and motivation fall into two categories: extrinsic and intrinsic.

Extrinsic rewards

When people think about rewards, they often immediately think of ones that are extrinsic: external, tangible forms of recognition, such as pay hikes, promotions, bonuses, and sales prizes. On the surface, extrinsic rewards tend to be easy to execute, such as "If you make your quota, we'll pay you $5,000." In fact, most organizations' established reward systems are built around such extrinsic rewards, and in some instances, they are effective, particularly in industries like sales, where bonuses can be linked to reaching certain quantitative goals. But many managers disagree with the notion that financial incentives are necessary to boost performance. Extrinsic rewards don't necessarily make people work harder or better. As Alfie Kohn writes in his widely cited HBR article, "Why Incentive Plans Cannot Work," "rewards typically undermine the very processes they are intended to enhance."

When such motivators do succeed, the positive effects are often short-lived. Money matters, certainly, and an organization will have a tough time recruiting and keeping good employees without a competitive level of pay and benefits. But while money can be a motivator, it does not build commitment and can also encourage the wrong behaviors, such as cutting ethical corners to earn a bonus or to game the reward system. And tensions can run high when monetary prizes are awarded for the results of a team. (See the sidebar "A Fair Approach to Financial Incentives.")

The biggest problem with extrinsic rewards, by far, is that while many people believe monetary compensation is a major driver of performance, research has found little evidence to back up that assumption. In fact, bonuses and other financial incentives in some cases can do more harm than good. "When it comes to producing lasting change in attitudes and behavior," writes Kohn, "rewards, like punishment, are strikingly ineffective. Once the rewards run out, people revert to their old behaviors." Extrinsic motivators don't change the attitudes that underlie behavior.

Unless you are a senior executive, you may not have much control over the financial and extrinsic rewards you can offer, but you do have the opportunity to provide intangible options that might mean more to your employees.

A FAIR APPROACH TO FINANCIAL INCENTIVES

In theory, it's easy to dole out cash when someone performs well. But in reality, it's not that simple.

Extrinsic rewards are quantifiable, but motivation is not. How much money does it take to alter someone's behavior? Offer $100 to your sales reps if they hit their quotas, and they won't bat an eye. Offer $1 million, and you'll have their full attention, but that's not a realistic figure. No one can say for certain what the right number is—and the right number for one person may be the wrong one for someone else.

What's more, it's rarely possible to sort out individual contributions to a project or determine what they're worth. Who should be rewarded when a new car is launched, for example? Should it be the designers, the engineers, the marketing team, or the executive who oversaw the whole project? Even if it were

(continued)

A FAIR APPROACH TO FINANCIAL INCENTIVES

possible to pinpoint the measure of any individual's contribution, this form of financial reward can actually undermine both teamwork and performance.

Most employees' main concern about pay-related issues is fairness, so if you do want to use financial incentives, make them fair and consistent. Concerns about fairness should not arise when the criteria of rewards are standard, based on clear metrics, and obvious to all—especially when individual contributors are the ones being rewarded.

But the issue of fairness is harder to resolve when rewarding members of a team. "Everyone on the team should participate in the reward payout," suggest Jeremy Hope and Steve Player in *Beyond Performance Management*. Since it's nearly impossible to determine and quantify the exact contribution of individuals on a team, don't try.

Intrinsic rewards

The opposite of extrinsic incentives, intrinsic rewards produce nonquantifiable personal satisfaction, such as a sense of accomplishment, personal control over one's work, and a feeling that efforts are appreciated. Examples include intellectual stimulation, skill development, autonomy, or challenge. When intrinsically motivated, people do things for their own sense of achievement because they inherently want to.

Intrinsic rewards must be thoughtfully tailored to individuals. A meaningful reward to one employee may not move another. A conscientious contributor might be thrilled to be given the opportunity to attend a conference in their area of interest, while an ambitious rising star might prefer being offered face time with the CEO or an appointment to a high-level project team.

There are a variety of ways that one can encourage good work through intrinsic rewards. Here are three tactics you can incorporate into your daily work, starting with recognition.

Acknowledge good work

Recognition is one of the most powerful tools in a manager's toolbox—and a far more powerful motivator than money. "Recognition is about feeling special," explains author and motivation expert Bob Nelson, and "it is hard to feel special from a corporate program where everyone gets the same thing, like a five-year pin."[4]

Each of your employees values recognition from a different audience. One person's favorite audience might be their peers, and that individual would appreciate public praise for their achievement in front of their colleagues. Someone more concerned with developing expertise might prize a professional or technical award. A person who prioritizes customer feedback above all would treasure a letter from a customer—or a photo of the employee and customer together, framed for their office wall. For an employee who cares most about your opinion, "the most powerful recognition would be a one-on-one conversation where you tell them quietly but vividly why they are such a valuable member of the team," suggests Marcus Buckingham in his HBR article "What Great Managers Do."

When deciding how to recognize individuals, take their personalities into account. An extrovert may get a kick out of a public display, but a more introverted person might cringe at such a spectacle. Tailor your approach to what you know of their preferences—and if you aren't sure, ask. The motivation employees derive from well-tailored recognition can be significant. In his article, Buckingham describes the example of Jim Kawashima, a Walgreens manager. Jim realized that his customer service representative, Manjit, was highly competitive and measurement focused—and she thrived on public recognition. So Jim covered his office walls with charts and figures highlighting employee successes in red. Because Manjit loved to win and see her successes acknowledged, she was driven to achieve the highest sales numbers on the team. Her success galvanized the rest of the staff, and after a few months their location was ranked first out of 4,000 in a companywide selling program.

Like feedback, recognition is best delivered frequently —at least once every other week. That may seem like a lot, but if your team gathers for weekly meetings, reserving a moment every other week to acknowledge an employee's contributions will take very little time and have a big impact.

As you think about ways to recognize good work, don't overlook the value of the written word. Consider copying your employee on an email to your boss highlighting their performance—or write a sincere thank-you note for exceptional work. During his tenure as president and CEO of Campbell Soup, Doug Conant wrote more than

30,000 individualized, handwritten thank-you notes to his 20,000 employees. Such thoughtful rewards and recognition can be deeply meaningful and highly motivating to your employees. Plus, they cost nearly nothing.

Provide decision-making discretion

As any entrepreneur can tell you, people are more motivated when they feel as though they own what they do. Employees are energized when they're empowered to make decisions that affect their own work. "Showing trust, granting autonomy, and recognizing the value of individual contributions all build employees' sense of ownership of their work and pride in performing it," says Monique Valcour, executive and career coach.[5] Giving your employees control over their work as their capabilities allow and supporting their efforts to achieve meaningful goals can lead to superior performance and can also serve as rich development opportunities. (We'll explore development further in the next section.)

Granting your employees the autonomy to make decisions increases their sense of ownership and control—and boosts their motivation. For example, Home Depot grants managers decision-making discretion over their own stores' merchandise and layout, rather than insisting that each outlet operate identically. Although the practice is less efficient financially, it keeps employees feeling engaged and rewarded.

Even if your organization doesn't spearhead efforts like these to empower employees, you can do the same on a smaller scale for your direct reports. Allow opportunities for each individual to operate more independently within their own work. If a representative is eager to improve the customer service experience, allow them to decide how best to do so, perhaps by surveying customers, running a focus group, digging into an established customer database, or with another approach you might not have thought of. When granted the freedom to choose how to tackle a project, your employee will likely feel a greater sense of ownership and engagement.

Introduce challenge

People are often capable of handling tasks that are more complex and more demanding than their managers expect and than their job descriptions require. Tackling such challenges can reward, inspire, and motivate them. In researching her book *Rookie Smarts: Why Learning Beats Knowing in the New Game of Work*, management consultant Liz Wiseman found that satisfaction increases as the level of challenge grows.

Consider giving employees higher-stakes assignments that involve more-complex problems or a bigger set of stakeholders. This could be a matter of offering a new work assignment or expanding a current one. For example, you could enlarge an employee's training session in coding to include participants from the entire organization rather than offering it to only those who are in their specific department. Depending on how big or challenging the project is, you may want to revisit the goals you and your employee agreed upon to account for the new challenge.

You can also invite your employees to stretch their skills and grow their expertise by giving them projects they've never done before—tasks where they haven't yet mastered all the relevant knowledge. This tactic may not work for every employee, however. "Make sure to choose people who have core aptitude or adjacent skills, but then let them learn as they go, Wiseman explains in her HBR.org article "An Easy Way to Make Your Employees Happier." "Their comfort zones will expand, and they'll take great pride in mastering new things." Remember, though, that the learning process can be rocky—and before someone feels comfortable with a new skill, they might feel frustrated or unsure for a while.

Finally, consider redirecting a person's existing expertise by pivoting to a new problem. Many skills are transferable from one area to another; with expertise in one field, some people can quickly pick up the nuances of a related one. For example, a scientist at a pharmaceutical company shifted her research from cellular biology—her area of expertise—to oncology. She was unsure, initially, about how to do so but after a few months reported feeling invigorated, challenged, and newly creative.

Recognizing your employees' good work and challenging them to do more can motivate them to continue exemplary work and contribute more to the organization. As you consider ways to encourage, engage, and build your direct reports' skills, think about what they may aspire to and how they want to grow in the long term—a key element of performance management called development that we'll cover in the next section.

NOTES

1. Gretchen Spreitzer and Christine Porath, "Creating Sustainable Performance," *Harvard Business Review*, January–February 2012 (product #R1201F).

2. Christine Porath and Christine Pearson, "The Price of Incivility," *Harvard Business Review*, January–February 2013 (product #R1301J).

3. Quoted in Gretchen Spreitzer and Christine Porath, "Creating Sustainable Performance," *Harvard Business Review*, January–February 2012 (product #R1201F).

4. Quoted in "Employee Recognition and Reward When Times Are Tough," *Harvard Management Update*, September 2003, https://hbr.org/2008/02/employee-recognition-and-rewar-1.html.

5. Monique Valcour, "The Power of Dignity in the Workplace," HBR.org, April 28, 2014 (product #H00S6P).

Developing Employees

CHAPTER 8

Understand Your Employee's Wants and Needs

Employee development is a process for managing a person's professional growth. Learning, building new skills, and working to one's full potential is both rewarding for the individual and helpful to the organization as a whole. For your direct reports, it means getting the opportunity to focus on their upward mobility. For you, it offers a chance to boost employees' productivity, motivation, and engagement while also retaining and growing your top talent.

Development is invaluable for your employees. Frederick Herzberg, in his classic HBR article "One More Time: How Do You Motivate Employees?" argues that growth is a powerful intrinsic motivator and can increase job satisfaction. Job seekers at all levels, from recent grads to executives, are more concerned with learning and development opportunities than with any other aspect of a prospective position. And in a study of Millennials in the workplace, professional services firm PwC found that training and development were the two most-valued benefits for these workers—even more than money, which ranked third.[1]

Companies whose employees are inspired and equipped to fulfill their greatest potential yield the best business results overall. And if high-performing individuals feel that they are regularly being given chances to grow, they will be more likely to stay with the organization, even during tough times. Likewise, having strong career development opportunities in place helps your organization prepare for the future; by giving them the training and skills they need, your employees will be ready to move into key roles when the opportunities arise.

Employee development, like motivating and coaching employees, should be an ongoing part of your performance management process. Tailor development efforts—which can include training, temporary "stretch" assignments, mentoring, and coaching, among other approaches—to the individual, and work with them to determine which ones are the right fit for their skills and aims.

Your Role in Employee Development

While development was once largely considered the domain of HR, it's actually every manager's responsibility to attend to their people's growth on an ongoing basis. Managers who take employee development seriously are more likely to lead a team with good morale and high standards, maintain a spirit of continuous improvement, and achieve better results.

Yet many managers are hesitant to develop their employees. Some argue that they don't have the time, especially if there are no challenging or interesting opportunities currently available for a direct report. Others find the conversations difficult if their employee isn't ready for promotion or if the manager doesn't have a clear plan of action in mind.

But neglecting development has consequences. Your employees may feel unsupported, and their morale and motivation may decline. Even your strongest performers can begin to feel stuck in their careers, and that increases the risk of them leaving the organization (see the sidebar "Preventing Career Plateaus"). Worse are the disillusioned, weaker performers who *don't* quit, leaving you with a destructive morale problem that can infect the culture.

PREVENTING CAREER PLATEAUS

Just because someone has strong skills and impressive performance doesn't mean they're happy in their job. In fact, psychologists Timothy Butler and James Waldroop write in their HBR article "Job Sculpting: The Art of Retaining Your Best People," "managers botch career development—and retention—because they mistakenly assume people are satisfied with jobs they excel at."

(continued)

PREVENTING CAREER PLATEAUS

Don't allow good people to get stuck in career plateaus. As a manager, you have a responsibility to make sure that the people you value are progressively advancing in their career paths.

How can you tell when someone is ready for a new challenge? They usually make it clear by asking or by pursuing development opportunities. But you can also watch for a few signs:

- Everything they manage has been running smoothly—for a significant period of time.

- When faced with problems, they jump quickly to solutions.

- They spend time trying to fix other people's and other departments' problems.

- While they're still performing well, they've become increasingly but inexplicably negative.

To retain your best performers and maintain their engagement, make an effort to offer meaningful development opportunities and challenges—and to raise the topic if they don't bring it up themselves.

On the other hand, people who are challenged and engaged describe their development process as exhilarating. When people are energized by learning, it's easy for them to stay engaged and perform at their peak. Satisfaction levels rise alongside challenge.

To be sure, investing in your direct reports' development takes time and thoughtful effort devoted to discussing and thinking about each of your employees and their futures. To best help your people develop, you'll need curiosity about each individual and patience for the learning process. But your employee will have to do the hard work of development—starting with taking ownership and embracing accountability for their own growth. You can't just hand your direct report a development plan and expect them to commit and run with it. Each employee's drive to grow needs to come from within. "Highly structured, one-size-fits-all learning programs don't work anymore," explains consultant and author Keith Ferrazzi. "Individuals must own, self-direct, and control their learning futures. Yet they can't do it alone, nor do you want them to."[2]

Start with the Employee

What do your direct reports want to learn? What are their career ambitions and interests, their passions and values? These aren't questions you can answer on your own. You're best off making ongoing career development a regular part of your conversations with your employees—but start with a comprehensive discussion about where they're headed.

Identify employee aspirations

A development-focused conversation can build rapport, help you connect on a personal level, and show your commitment to helping your direct report grow while you gather useful information. Your frequent discussions about an employee's performance and progress toward goals may naturally lead to conversations about their career aspirations—but if the topic doesn't arise naturally, ask directly. Give your employee a heads-up that you'd like to talk about their career plans and future development so they can reflect beforehand.

Your goal in the discussion is to understand your employee's aspirations as well as their current state of workplace know-how and daily performance. Explore their current developmental level and goals (for example, what they are ready for, how much more work they can handle, what the next step should be in their journey), their learning style and preferences, and their motivations and values. What makes your employee tick? What is it that they're after? Recognition? A raise or promotion? Autonomy? Aim to identify what your direct report wants to achieve most both in the short term and in their long-term career.

To elicit information, ask open-ended questions rather than ones that require a simple yes or no response, and practice active listening (see the sidebar "Be an Active Listener" in chapter 5). Some sample questions you can use are:

- What do you want to be known for?

- What matters most to you?

- What do you see yourself doing a year from now that you're not currently doing?

- What does success look like for you?

- Where and when do you feel you are at your personal best?

- What's your favorite part of what you do?

- Where would you like to be in your career in three, five, or 10 years?

While you may have discussed some of these aspirations and interests in your goal-setting meeting—or even in your feedback and coaching sessions—ambitions can shift over time. When it comes to development, revisiting these topics ensures that you and your direct report will choose a productive path to meaningful growth.

By better understanding your employee's personal and learning goals, you'll both be in a stronger position to identify developmental opportunities.

Align ambitions with organizational needs

Match an individual's interests, values, and skills to growth opportunities based on their level of performance and potential. You'll want to find a development path that is meaningful to your employee to ensure their commitment, but work toward an overlap between what will bring them the most satisfaction *and* what will be best for the organization.

Erika Andersen, founding partner of the coaching, consulting, and training firm Proteus and author of *Be Bad First*, suggests focusing on three questions to help choose a direction for your employee:

- **What will drive the economic engine?** Identify capabilities that provide value to the organization. For example, someone in operations could reduce cycle and delivery times by learning how to better manage complex custom client projects, reduce expenses by learning more about sourcing materials, or boost productivity by setting and communicating clearer direction for their own direct reports. Jot down or make a mental note of all the options to choose from.

- **What is the individual best at?** Once you and your direct report have identified useful capacities that they might develop, consider whether they can excel at them by assessing their innate strengths. Are they good at performing other, similar tasks? Someone who is organized and sequential in how they approach work may easily grasp complex project management—and they could better share that thinking with their team by mastering some communication and management skills. But if they struggle with research, learning to excel at sourcing materials may be more difficult.

- **What is the individual passionate about?** After assessing where an employee's strengths overlap with valuable areas for potential development, think back to your discussion about their aspirations. Identify how interested they are in those areas. Strengths are not just things that we're good at but things that can energize us as well. Perhaps your employee perks up at the idea of managing complex projects, but the very prospect of leading a team sounds draining to them. Development efforts work best when they feel exciting, not burdensome, so capitalize on your employees' interests by helping them choose a path that energizes them.

Rethink the Traditional Promotion Track

As you think about a direction for your employee, consider their career trajectory. A traditional path of advancement may not make sense given a direct report's interests, skills, and ambitions.

A long-trusted concept in career development has been the career ladder: a logical series of stages that move a talented and promotable employee upward through progressively more challenging and responsible positions. But clear career ladders are less common in the rapidly changing, sometimes unpredictable world of contemporary work. Simple and straightforward career paths are harder to identify as hierarchical structures break down and organizations flatten. In some fields and companies, the traditional ladder model has shifted to what Deloitte vice chairman and managing principal Cathy Benko calls a "lattice." In the case of a lattice, people shift roles, responsibilities, and even business areas over the course of their careers, sometimes more than once.

"In the industrial era the corporate ladder was the standard metaphor for talent development and career paths. Its one-size-fits-all, only-way-is-up rules were clear, and incentives uniformly supported them," Benko notes in her coauthored HBR article "AT&T's Talent Overhaul." "The lattice, in contrast, represents career paths that change continually and adaptively through multidirectional, zigzag movements."

In the ladder model, career paths were clearly delineated—an editorial assistant who is promoted to assistant editor, to associate editor, and finally to editor—and headed one way: upward. But the multidirectional lattice model allows for greater flexibility: an editorial assistant who discovers an interest in video production develops those visual and technical skills, and through apprenticeships and training opportunities shifts from a text-heavy role in their organization's book-publishing division to a multimedia-focused position in its e-learning branch. With the lattice, employees can move laterally or diagonally; they can ascend or descend.

This may require a shift in thinking as you consider what your employee's direction may be in the organization. Preparing a direct report and shaping their skills to fit a traditional role in management may be a mismatch if they'd prefer another position that taps into their strengths and interests.

Instead of putting each of your employees on the same track of automatic advancement (once they've learned the appropriate skills, of course), think about their career aspirations. What does your direct report most want to do or be? Whether they hunger to become a manager, want to expand an exciting aspect of the current role they generally enjoy, or yearn to learn a new skill that overlaps with another department, identify a direction that meets your employee's personal needs as well as those of the organization, even in the long term.

Once you and your direct report have identified their wants and needs and pinpointed a specific direction or area they should develop, don't jump right into action. There are a variety of ways that they can grow their skills. For example, you might sign them up for training programs, introduce new challenges in their daily work, or let them try a temporary new assignment. Carefully consider the options available to you and what may work best with your employee. We'll explore potential development tactics in the next chapter.

NOTES

1. "Millennials Survey. Millennials at Work: Reshaping the Workplace," PwC, http://www.pwc.com/gx/en/issues/talent/future-of-work/millennials-survey.html.

2. Keith Ferrazzi, "7 Ways to Improve Employee Development Programs," HBR.org, July 31, 2015 (product #H028T9).

CHAPTER 9

Expand Your Employee's Skill Sets

Once you've decided on a direction for a motivated employee's development, you'll need to figure out how they'll acquire the skills to get them there. There are many approaches to growing your employee's capabilities, from short-term training options that help them stay up-to-date on the latest industry knowledge to encouraging them to foster career-shaping, long-term relationships. The right approach will be determined by the employee's situation and preferences. Consider the following tactics as potential options for development.

Skill-Training Programs

In many fields, learning and development have a short shelf life. In industries that are constantly changing and innovating, skills can become obsolete within mere months. Staying current in emerging technology, for example, requires a perpetual learning effort.

Some companies offer "corporate universities" as a way for their employees to learn the latest in their industry and job. These programs let a company tailor the curriculum to align training with its particular business strategy, focusing on the specific skills needed for organizational success. As a manager, you'll know whether these options are available to your employees (and if you don't, you can always ask your HR department). If you work in a particularly highly regulated field, like accounting, this traditional classroom training approach can work well.

These formal programs can be time-consuming, though, and they can take employees temporarily off the job. In some rapidly advancing fields—cloud-based computing, coding, and data science, for example—the curriculum changes so fast that traditional training methods can't keep up.

In cases like these, consider more-flexible options. Encourage your employees to pursue off-site education at local schools or universities—or through online classes, which are usually less expensive than campus-based training and require no in-person class time. Online courses, certifications, and degree and "nanodegree" programs are widely available, regardless of geographic location, through university-developed MOOCs (massive open online courses) and e-learning companies (like Coursera, Lynda.com, and Udemy). You can help your employees find such programs by looking online at reputable sources and courses that provide the skills your team members need at a pace that works for them. If price is an issue, talk to your HR department to see if your organization offers tuition assistance for employees to invest in their growth.

Task Delegation

You may discover that an employee could learn better on the job than in the classroom. Task delegation allows you to test and expand their skills by handing off specific work assignments without adding these new responsibilities to their job permanently.

In this development tactic, you hand off a task (either yours or someone else's) to your employee to gauge their ability in the project and offer more challenge. When you delegate one of your responsibilities to a direct report, you transfer not only the work but also the accountability for completing it—which builds trust. Delegating is an excellent way to communicate your confidence in your direct report's ability. In doing so, you're saying "I'm confident you can get the job done."

Every time you hand off a project or task, you're giving someone an opportunity to test their skills in mastering a new challenge. In some cases, this gives them experience with managerial work, like learning how to accept responsibility, to plan work, and to enlist the collaboration of others. In any case, it's especially important to monitor their progress, offer feedback, and coach as needed to be sure that they're learning the new skill.

Stretch Assignments

An alternative to delegation is to provide a discrete, time-limited stretch assignment. This is a particularly helpful method to assess whether an employee who has expressed interest in being promoted is truly ready for a more challenging role. Rather than handing off a task from your to-do list, design an assignment similar to what the person would handle in their potential new role. The key is for them to perform tasks they don't necessarily know how to do or that they can't yet do well.

Suitable temporary assignments for ambitious employees could include:

- Asking your direct report to develop and launch a product or head up a new initiative or project.

- Giving an employee the opportunity to fix a business or product that's in trouble, like improving the bottom line of a new service or marketing a struggling product to a new customer segment.

- Assigning a job rotation in a new work environment. For example, have a marketing manager work in the sales organization for a while, offer an employee a short-term foreign assignment, or encourage your employee to join an organization-wide committee.

- Creating distinct tours of duty, where an employee takes over a new role for a specific time period before moving on to another role. (To learn more about this option, refer to the sidebar "Tours of Duty.")

For this type of development opportunity, it's especially important to be transparent about what you're doing. Ensure that this is a short-term experiment, not a permanent change in responsibilities, and assign clear criteria for success and a time line for evaluation.

TOURS OF DUTY

Effectively a contract between a manager and an employee, a tour of duty is an arrangement in which an employee agrees to take on a new role for only a short amount of time. This tactic recognizes that lifelong employment and loyalty are no longer realistic expectations in today's work world. Few individuals will stay at any organization for the entirety of their career—but chances are good that they will stay for a few years, especially with a targeted set of goals to achieve.

A tour of duty can serve as a personalized retention plan that gives an employee concrete, compelling reasons to finish their tour and establishes a clear time frame for discussing their future at the organization. As a manager, you can construct customized tours that are mutually beneficial for the employee and your organization, with explicit terms, clear expectations, time-limited commitments, and focused goals.

When Reid Hoffman founded LinkedIn, he set the expectation for a four-year tour for each of his employees with discussions to be held after two years. If an employee produced tangible achievements for the firm during those four years, the company would

(continued)

TOURS OF DUTY

help them advance their career—either inside or beyond the company. One successful tour was likely to lead to another. The two- to four-year period syncs with typical product development cycles in the software business, though other industries also operate on similar schedules.

The end of the tour need not be the end of an employee's tenure with your organization, though. Instead, it can be the beginning of another tour offering another opportunity—for example, reengineering a business process, developing and launching a new product, or spearheading an organizational innovation.

As a manager, you may be assigning your employees to tours where you don't have oversight. In cases like these, you'll want to keep in regular contact with the individual to assess progress and growth and check in with their supervisor to get their point of view. This is especially important if you'd like them to return to your team in some capacity after their tour of duty.

Job Redesign

Job redesign allows a promising employee the opportunity to try their hand at a new task while changing the job permanently. Here, you make adjustments to an individual's role at the margins, reassigning rote, lower-level tasks to employees for whom the tasks are more appropriate (or eliminating the items altogether). You then replace these tasks with higher-level ones that involve challenge and learning. For example, if a direct report whose work is mainly administrative demonstrates an interest in copywriting, you may be able to shift some of their administrative duties to the department assistant, freeing up some time for them to take on introductory writing projects.

The starting point for redesign is a careful inventory of all the tasks associated with the job. You and your direct report may be able to compile a list from their formal job description, from their to-do list, or through information gathered during check-ins and ongoing performance discussions. Look for opportunities to offload low-level items, perhaps to another team member or administrative staffer. Keep in mind, though, that just because someone has always done a task doesn't mean that it is worth doing; you may identify out-of-date or unnecessary activities that can be eliminated altogether, such as pulling weekly analytics reports for the team when an automated monthly report is doing the trick. Then identify and add a more challenging assignment in its place as a regular part of the job.

Job redesign may be easiest when working within a team. Can you find your direct report a partner with complementary strengths to take on the tasks you want to hand off? It takes effort to custom fit a role to better suit an individual, but doing so will save you time in the long run. When people slave away at tasks that don't suit them, they (and by extension you) rarely get good results. People are far more energized, efficient, and effective when their responsibilities draw on their innate strengths and abilities.

If you believe that someone can contribute at a higher level, don't simply pile on new responsibilities. An "invisible" promotion that doesn't recognize a person's contributions with a corresponding raise or change in title can sap motivation. It can also lead to employee burnout. Instead, investigate how you can create a better fit between an employee's work and their best self. Consider what they do well and find intrinsically satisfying and how they can do more of it. Great managers tailor roles so that individuals can succeed in their own way, capitalizing on their strengths and neutralizing weaknesses.

For example, in his HBR article "What Great Managers Do," author and consultant Marcus Buckingham writes about Michelle, a Walgreens manager, who successfully tweaked the role of her employee, Jeffrey, to capitalize on his strengths. Not much of a people person, Jeffrey excelled when given clear, specific tasks, like stocking an aisle with new items and revising displays. In most Walgreens stores, one person is responsible for a particular aisle, including arranging the merchandise. But to capitalize on Jeffrey's gift for precision, Michelle made Jeffrey's entire job stocking and arranging products—in every aisle—while handing off his more social responsibilities to other coworkers. Jeffrey was able to spend his time on a task he excelled at and enjoyed while taking his sub-par people skills out of the spotlight. What's more, by shifting around tasks on the team, his more social colleagues were relieved of work they considered a chore and could focus more of their time on what they did best: serving customers. After the role reorganization, Michelle saw increases in the store's sales, profits, and customer satisfaction, and Jeffrey's confidence grew so much that he became interested in management roles.

Capitalizing on individual employees' unique abilities in this way can also help strengthen your team. Colleagues can recognize and better appreciate one another's strengths while their coworkers fill in to neutralize their weaknesses.

It's worth noting that it's not always realistic for someone to hand off tasks and responsibilities they don't love. If one team member drops an item from their list that doesn't bring out their very best, another team member will have to pick it up. In some instances, particularly as people are taking on more and more work, there isn't always someone who can pick up the discarded task—in which case you should consider other development options.

Mentorship and Sponsorship

Beyond course work and challenging tasks, employees can grow by tapping into the support and expertise of others around them. Mentors are individuals with experience, knowledge, skills, and perspective, who work one-on-one with employees to help them discover ways to achieve their goals. According to management consultant Tamara Erickson, "A good mentor is part diagnostician, assessing what's going on with you now, and part guide, connecting you with the advice, ideas, people, and resources you need to grow and move ahead."[1]

Mentors teach, advise, motivate, and inspire and can provide guidance, career help, and even coaching to boost professional and personal development. They can help your employees meet challenges by offering encouragement and providing valuable feedback about where to improve. Given their experience and expertise in the company and their job, they can be valuable role models who help others understand and navigate organizational politics as well as help build support networks. While you may not play an active role in the mentoring relationship for your employees, you can help them align with the right type of mentor and assist them in managing the relationship.

Mentorship is not just for ambitious early career upstarts; people at all stages of their careers can benefit from mentorship. Different types of mentors will be appropriate in different stages of a person's career.

- **Buddy or peer mentors** are suitable in the early stages of an employee's work life, when what is most helpful is a peer-based mentor who can speed up the learning curve. This type of mentor can provide assistance and information about skill development and basic organization-specific practices. Such mentoring relationships can come about somewhat informally, through social and professional networks.

- **Career mentors** serve as career advisors and advocates for employees after their initial period at an organization. This mentor helps provide context and explains how an individual's contri-

butions fit into the bigger picture and purpose of
the organization. Author and CEO Anthony Tjan
explains, "When people feel that they understand
their current role, its impact, and where it can take
them next in a company, it leads to higher levels of
satisfaction and motivation."[2] This type of mentor should be a supportive advocate and advisor
within the company and should meet with their
mentee semiannually or quarterly.

- **Life mentors** offer invaluable support for people in
the mid- and senior stages of their careers. Tjan
explains that people at this point need "someone in
whom they can confide without feeling that there
is any bias. This is someone who can be a periodic
sounding board when one is faced with a difficult
career challenge, or when they are considering
changing jobs." While life mentors don't supplant
career or peer mentors, they can impart significant
wisdom and should be consulted annually.

- **Sponsors** are like mentors, but rather than solely
focusing on support, they also advocate for an
employee. As economist and author Sylvia Ann
Hewlett explains, "Where a mentor might help you
envision your next position, a sponsor will advocate for your promotion and lever open the door."[3]
Sponsors can spur a protégé's career into corporate
heights by connecting employees to senior leaders, promoting their visibility, opening up career
opportunities, helping them network outside
the company, and generally providing advice.

These individuals are usually two levels above the employee, with a line of sight into potential future roles.

Employees shouldn't be limited to one single mentor or sponsor. Instead, they would be better served by a "developmental network" with various areas of expertise and different perspectives. Tapping into multiple supports decreases the likelihood of wearing out one individual mentor or sponsor, or finding oneself without guidance if that person leaves the company or is unavailable. A mentoring relationship can be a long-term, even lifelong, relationship—or it can last just a few hours or weeks.

As a manager, you may be able to introduce your employee to mentors and sponsors who can turbocharge their career development. But where do you find them? Some companies offer formal programs that encourage mentorship. If your organization has no formal program in place, ask your employee what they're looking for in a mentoring relationship to see if you know anyone who might be the right fit. You might consider looking for mentors or sponsors who:

- Are able to understand and shape the employee's long-term professional goals, such as someone who has a similar background, or someone in a position the employee might like to have in the future.

- Are influential within the organization. These individuals know how things work and can help your direct report navigate the system.

- Have a broader skill set than your employee, so they can help them grow and develop in new ways.

- Possess a higher level of functional experience than your employee does. Sometimes this is a person outside your organization or outside the chain of command, like someone in a trade organization.

- Are not part of your organization and therefore may be able to offer broader perspectives and provide even better support for ambitious employees.

You may also want to discuss with your direct report some basics they should establish at the beginning of the relationship. For example, How often should they meet? What types of things should they discuss? What are their expectations for confidentiality? While you can take some steps to set your employee up for success, it is in their hands to secure and maintain the mentoring relationship once it's established.

All of these development tactics can help individuals cultivate the skills they need in order to reach their professional aspirations, but remember that your employees are unique and learn in their own ways. If you want your direct report's development efforts to be effective, you need to decide which option best meets their personal learning style and then craft a plan for paving the way to success.

NOTES

1. Tamara Erickson, "Introduction: Taking Charge of Your Career," in *HBR Guide to Getting the Mentoring You Need*, Harvard Business Review Press, 2014, 1.

2. Anthony K. Tjan, "Keeping Great People with Three Kinds of Mentors," HBR.org, August 12, 2011 (product #H007LK).

3. Sylvia Ann Hewlett, "The Right Way to Find a Career Sponsor," HBR.org, September 11, 2013, https://hbr.org/2013/09/the-right-way-to-find-a-career-sponsor.

CHAPTER 10

Craft a Development Plan

Skill training, job redesign, mentorship—your employee could take advantage of all of the development options available to them, but without a strategic plan, they still might not achieve their professional goals and aspirations. You must clearly identify a path that you both think will work best and outline the specific actions required to gain the skills they need to grow. In other words, you and your employee must define a development plan.

An individualized development plan includes specific growth objectives your employee will strive to meet over the long term, with a time line and clear steps for achieving them. Like the performance goals you developed in section 1, these targets should be challenging but achievable. After all, if the employee isn't required to stretch or push themselves, they won't grow.

Just as goals are best crafted in collaboration with an employee, so are individualized plans for development. The action steps that you identify should take into account your employee's professional aims (which you explored in chapter 8) as well as organizational needs. You'll also likely want to include some of the development tactics covered in the last chapter. In order to do so, though, you must first understand how your employee learns best. Then you can craft a plan—and implement it in a way that ensures they will follow through.

Understand Your Employee's Learning Style

Not all development options work for everyone. An effective mode of learning for one person can fall flat for another. Personality type, education, and cultural background all influence the way individuals learn, and with five generations of people in the workplace, organizations need to match training and development tools to employees' preferences. For example, digital-native Millennials may gravitate to online learning or other tech-based approaches, while employees of other generations may prefer on-the-job learning opportunities such as mentorship or stretch assignments.

In his HBR article "What Great Managers Do," author and consultant Marcus Buckingham identifies three learning styles—analyzing, doing, and watching—that are worth considering when you're planning which tactics to use for your employees' development. These styles are not mutually exclusive, and in fact, some of your direct reports may rely on a combination of two or perhaps all three.

1. **Analyzing.** An analyzer craves information. They understand a task by taking it apart into components, examining each element, and reconstructing it. An analyzer prefers to fully prepare before doing, so assigned reading, classroom experience, and role-play are effective ways for them to learn new skills.

2. **Doing.** A doer learns more during a given activity than through preparation. Trial and error is an integral part of their learning process, as they tend to enhance their skills while grappling with tasks. For a doer, it's best to pick a specific action that is simple but real, give them a brief overview of the results you want, and get out of their way. As they develop, gradually increase the degree of difficulty until they've mastered the role.

3. **Watching.** A watcher prefers to see a task or project from start to finish so they can understand what the total performance looks like. They want to see how everything fits together in a coherent whole. It's best to avoid classroom learning and how-to manuals for this type of learner. Instead, consider shadowing opportunities in which they can observe someone in the act.

Work with your employee to define how they perform best, and ask questions to get to the heart of their learning style. Once you identify their preferences, don't try to change them. Forcing your employee into a path that doesn't fit just causes frustration. Accept the uniqueness of each individual, and develop a plan that takes into account how they think and what drives them.

Craft a Plan

Outlining your employee's development plan requires time and collaborative discussion with your direct report. You may need to meet a few times before the plan is finalized to ensure agreement.

Ask your employee to draft an initial outline, and have them explain why they selected certain options. People are more engaged in plans they have some choice in creating, and allowing them to start the discussion will let them incorporate their own learning styles and preferences. If they need help pulling a plan together, ask questions like:

- Who can help and support you in learning how to become proficient at this task?

- How can I support you in figuring out how to do this on your own?

- How will we measure the success of this target?

Make suggestions if necessary, but allow your employee to choose which learning options they want to pursue.

Don't limit your employee to just one avenue for growth. For example, the 70–20–10 rule, also known as the "experience, exposure, education" framework, suggests making at least 70% of the action items on-the-job learning through stretch assignments, 20% from mentoring, and 10% from formal training or educational programs. An employee's plan might involve adding one or two challenging assignments, complemented with coaching and formal skill training. The right approach will be determined by the individual's situation and what they think they can handle.

Next, figure out what resources are needed. Perhaps your direct report needs a private work space to participate in an online course, a subscription for new software they're trying to master, or a conference registration fee paid from a corporate account. Maybe they need you to introduce them to potential mentors or sponsors. Consider the resources required for your direct report to successfully complete their development plan. If you can't afford or provide the necessary resources, reassess the plan and discuss other alternatives.

Throughout your conversations, talk with your direct report about what, if anything, their development efforts mean for their pay and position. They may have questions about what job redesign or a stretch assignment will mean in the long term. Be clear about whether this is a new job or a change in responsibilities, a promotion, or a trial assignment. Development may or may not lead to an adjustment in salary or status, but your employee should understand from the start what's in store.

Whatever options you and your direct report agree will spur their development—whether it's a one-day seminar, an online course, or a task delegated from your own to-do list—agree on a time line for completion, or highlight specific milestones if the development is an on-going relationship, as with mentoring. Without set deadlines, your employee won't have a clear idea of the time commitment their development requires.

Document Your Decisions— and Follow Up

Get the final plan on paper. If your company has an individual development plan form, use that to make a record of your discussions. If not, create your own, using table 10-1 at the end of this chapter as a template.

As with other parts of performance management, your conversation with your employee isn't the end of the process. Schedule specific times to discuss how their development is going. Choose a date a month or so away, or fold these conversations into your regular check-ins and feedback discussions.

Don't get frustrated if your direct report isn't growing as quickly as you'd hoped. Learning is a messy process, and development doesn't always follow a straight line. As a manager, you'll need to have the patience to allow people to make mistakes. Your employees need to feel safe to explore and experiment if they are to take risks in learning and mastering new skills.

Few individuals will risk stretching to meet an ambitious target if they're not sure their manager has their back. Let your employees know you trust them to take on new challenges—and to recover from missteps. Ensure that they feel safe taking risks for growth as they do their jobs. Developing and maintaining a safe working environment requires ongoing discussion of needs and opportunities, tasks and obstacles—what is working and what is not.

Allowing your direct reports to learn and explore pays off: As individuals achieve small successes, their confidence grows, so they're less daunted by bigger challenges. Step back to allow self-sufficiency, and let your employees own their results. Once you've delegated a task or decision, don't try to take it back. Encourage each person to learn through their mistakes, and recognize and reward them when they succeed. If you do find that someone is struggling to the point of frustration or in a way that is detrimental to their performance, work with that person to make adjustments so that they can find the path that's right for them.

TABLE 10-1

Individual development plan template

List three primary development goals that the individual aims to accomplish. Include a description of how those goals will be measured or the expected outcomes.

Development goals	Measures of achievement/expected outcomes
1.	
2.	
3.	

Development goal 1:

Tactic for development:

Choose skill training, task delegation, stretch assignments, or mentoring and sponsorships.

Describe the assignment:

Tasks required for the assignment and plans to meet them:

Estimated time frame with milestones:

Development goal 2:

Tactic for development:

Choose skill training, task delegation, stretch assignments, or mentoring and sponsorships.

Describe the assignment:

Tasks required for the assignment and plans to meet them:

Estimated time frame with milestones:

TABLE 10-1 *(continued)*

Development goal 3:

Tactic for development:

Choose skill training, task delegation, stretch assignments, or mentoring and sponsorships.

Describe the assignment:

Tasks required for the assignment and plans to meet them:

Estimated time frame with milestones:

Resources needed

What additional support or resources are needed to achieve the employee's goals? How will it be provided?

Monitoring progress

How often will the employee and manager meet to discuss progress? List any upcoming dates.

Time frame

Start date of plan: Anticipated completion date:

This plan is agreed to as indicated by the signatures below.

_____   _____
Employee signature   Date

_____   _____
Manager signature   Date

Source: Adapted from *Pocket Mentor: Developing Employees* (Boston: Harvard Business Press, 2009), 75–76.

CHAPTER 11

How to Develop Someone Who's Struggling

Every organization has a range of performers, from thriving stars to those who are struggling. On one end of the spectrum are the A players, the top 10% of the workforce whose contributions are exceptional. The steadily contributing B players do good work and generally form the solid backbone of units and departments. These two groups make up the vast majority of your workforce and consistently deliver strong performance.

On the bottom 10%, though, are your C players. These individuals produce work that is just barely acceptable. These aren't generally strong contributors who simply struggle with one part of their job but rather employees who consistently underdeliver and don't provide the results your team and organization need.

It's tempting to ignore this group of employees—or summarily dismiss them from the company. After all, shouldn't managers spend most of their time and energy working with the people who add the most value? Failing to develop your C players' skills outright, though, comes with its own set of downfalls. These individuals often:

- Stand in the way of advancement of more-talented employees

- Hire other C players, which lowers the performance bar across the board.

- Tend to be poor role models who encourage a low-performer mentality among their peers and direct reports

- Engender a culture of mediocrity that repels highly talented and ambitious people away from your team and organization

What's more, replacing an employee is a time-consuming task—and even a stellar new hire will need a period of training and acclimation before adding much value. So while it's true that in some cases firing a C player may be the best choice, it's rarely the place to start. You owe it to yourself and your organization—as well as the underperforming employee—to diagnose and address the underlying causes of poor performance.

Consider the three Cs of dealing with C players—converse, coach, and can—coined by John Baldoni, chair of leadership development at the global leadership advisory firm N2Growth.

Converse: Identify What's Causing the Issue

To solve the problem, you must first find the root cause. Four issues commonly underlie poor performance:

- **Lack of clarity.** Does your employee know what you expect of them?

- **Poor effort.** Is your employee investing enough time and energy into the work?

- **No sense of strategy.** Do they approach their work with an organized plan?

- **Underwhelming talent.** Do they have the skills, knowledge, and capabilities to do the job well?

To determine the cause of underperformance, collect the right information. Establish the details of the unsatisfactory work: What is the person doing or not doing? Gather your facts and observations before discussing the problem with the underperformer. Much like you would do in preparation for a feedback conversation, find out what their peers, supervisors, and direct reports have to say—but do so in confidence. Think, too, about the competencies required for the job. Does the employee have the necessary skills to perform the job effectively?

Ask yourself whether you're contributing to the problem. Were you unclear in your expectations? Did you provide your direct report the resources and freedom to complete their job? It's also worth delving into your own assumptions about the employee, which may be unduly negative. Perhaps there are certain types of tasks they do well, or maybe they contributed satisfactorily to particular projects, but you didn't see these instances because you were only focused on their flaws. What skills or qualities allowed them to perform well in these cases? If you can identify your direct report's strengths in these situations, it may be possible to replicate the conditions that made them successful in other areas of work. Even if good performance is the exception rather than the rule, the person may be worth keeping around.

Personal issues—for example, health or family problems, or even a disruptive move to a new house—can also temporarily throw someone off their game and keep them from devoting their normal level of attention to work. If you notice underperformance from someone with a history of good work, check to see if personal problems may be the cause. Such employees are worth saving, so try to find a way to work around the issue.

Consider the example of Philippe, Allie's employee who struggled to turn in complete, timely, and correct budgets. Allie had brought up the issue a few times before, but the problems persisted. To get the full picture, Allie referred to her notes about the problem from previous feedback conversations and touched base with a few of her colleagues to see if they'd had similar issues.

But Allie didn't stop there. She thought hard about her own role. She felt she had set up the right expectations for Philippe, but he still struggled to submit the budgets in a timely manner. Philippe was a team player and showed strength in other aspects of his role, but completing these regular budgets was an integral part of his job. Allie concluded that Philippe was worth taking the time to develop and change.

Once you've seen the problem from a number of angles, present the employee with the facts of what you observe, providing frank and honest feedback, and—if the person demonstrates willingness—creating a plan for improvement and development.

Coach: Work Toward Improvement

Before sitting down with your direct report, give them advance notice that you'd like to discuss their performance and development. When you meet, describe the problematic behavior and the impact it's having on the rest of the team. Review the specific details of the issue—don't just describe the problem in general terms. For example, Allie might say to Philippe, "You've been late submitting your last few budgets, and I've found some troubling errors when I reviewed them. There are some basic errors that look like a matter of attention to detail, but it takes a lot of my time to review and make sense of them. And when you don't submit them on time, it requires that my assistant figure out whose budget is missing and then track you down to find out the status. This interferes with the other work she needs to complete."

Just as you would when delivering feedback, refer to the context of the problem, if applicable. "This is not the first time we've had to talk about this. According to my records, we discussed this problem last quarter and last year. Yet the problem continues." Be explicit about how they should improve: "These budgets must be corrected and submitted by deadline for you to remain a member of this team and organization."

While this straightforward approach may be hard for your direct report to hear, assure them that you want to help. Consider these sample phrases:

- "I'm seeing issues with your performance, and I believe that you can do better. So how do we improve?"

- "What adjustments might we try that would help you achieve your goals?"

- "What can I do to help you be more effective?"

Showing your support will help your employee sidestep feelings of defensiveness and be more willing to correct course.

Assess their willingness to change

No matter how hard you try, you can't force-feed something that is ultimately the employee's responsibility. Before devoting resources to develop low performers, assess whether they're committed to their own improvement.

Once you've explained the problem at hand, listen actively to the employee's response to determine whether or not they're open to engaging on the issue. Do they get defensive, make excuses, or claim that their performance is in fact adequate? Or do they provide useful information about the causes behind the issues you've raised? Perhaps their poor work is due to inadequate resources, whether it's staff, budget, time, or managerial support, or maybe they are struggling to understand expectations or build the skills necessary for the job. Maybe they're being affected by someone else's poor performance—for example, being delayed by one of their direct reports who isn't delivering *their* complete and correct budget statements on time.

Allie took note of Philippe's tone and body language as he spoke. He didn't seem surprised by her comments, though he did seem hesitant to give her the full story. Allie pressed to get more information, and he explained that he felt uncertain about the budgets, and even if his team members submitted their information on time, the budgets were often late because he was worried he was submitting them incorrectly, based on their previous discussions. He was unable to spot the problems, but just knowing they were there made him nervous and led to his delay in sending them.

Your preparatory work and active listening will help you distinguish between responses that are true explanations and those that are defensive excuses for bad performance. Honest responses indicate that a person is open to change. When an underperformer demonstrates concern about the problem and a willingness to make an effort toward improvement, work with them to develop a specific plan. If your employee does not show an interest in change, you may need to consider other alternatives to development.

Create a plan for improvement

With a willing employee, state your firm expectations for improvement clearly, and, together, craft a concrete plan for change. Be explicit: What will each of you do differently? What measurable actions will mark progress along the way? In many cases, performance issues arise from a mismatch between a manager's expectations and those of an employee. Write a list of the employee's three most-important responsibilities, and ask them to do the same. Then compare your results. You may find that, with some alignment of expectations and continuing discussion through your ongoing check-in conversations, your direct report can soon be on the right track.

While in many aspects of performance management it's helpful for an employee to draft an initial plan for improvement in order to increase their sense of ownership, for an underperformer you should be more directive. Provide a specific request with clear timelines, and then check for understanding. For example, Allie told Philippe, "What I'd suggest is that you set a quarterly reminder a few weeks before your budget is due to ask your team members to finish the components they're responsible for, and block out a window to compile the data and go over any questions with them. Then you'll be able to submit complete and clear budgets on time, and we won't have to have another of these conversations."

This discussion provides an opportunity for you to consider the various development options available to your employee. Philippe might do well with some online training or a refresher course—on budgeting, perhaps, or in Excel. If he has a colleague who consistently delivers polished, error-free budgets, Allie might connect them to discuss best practices for preparation. Perhaps the problem is less about the budget than about Philippe's management of his own direct reports, and if so, leadership training or mentorship might be more helpful to him. Whatever you decide, keep a record of your discussions and what plan you've agreed to.

Follow up

Schedule regular meetings to talk about progress—or ask the person to check in with you periodically. (If they don't follow up on this, they may not truly be willing to work to improve.)

For example, Allie sent Philippe to a half-day course on budgeting so he could better identify errors in his budgets and those of his direct reports. She scheduled a meeting a few weeks before the next budget was due to review the information he had at that point and explain any problems with what he'd put together. They met a few times over the course of the next weeks before he was able to submit a final, error-free budget. Allie also offered Philippe some feedback and guidance about how he might address one of his employees who consistently submitted incomplete information.

It was a time-intensive intervention, but the regular meetings paid off: Philippe's next budget was complete, correct, and turned in on time. He showed clear improvement as well as motivation to continue to improve next time. "I think I have a better handle on the process now," he said, "but just in case, can we plan to review a draft of my budget in advance of next quarter's deadline?"

In addition to these follow-up meetings, provide your employee with real-time feedback. Praise positive change, and pay attention to development and improvement. Make it clear that you notice and appreciate the results of their hard work.

Cut: Know When to Let Go

It can take a while for people to change their behavior and improve their performance, so don't expect an overnight transformation. For coaching and development efforts to work, your employee must also have the capacity to get to the necessary skill level. If your employee is enthusiastic but not showing even incremental progress toward targets, find out more about why this is happening. Let them know that they're not meeting your expectations, and ask questions to get their perspective. You could say, for example, "The needle hasn't moved on these skills we've identified as important. Were the expectations we set earlier too high or unrealistic? Is there a different way that you can learn this?" You could consider bringing in a third party, perhaps even another team member, to coach in your place.

If the employee continues to underperform, you'll need to decide if they are the right person for this role, task, or responsibility. If they demonstrate willingness, you might redirect them to work that calls on the skills they do have, whether by shifting their role or changing particular assignments.

Alternatively, if they are unwilling to improve or are just meeting the base needs of the position, you'll need to take decisive action. Address issues as they arise to communicate urgency. Shift your focus from eliciting improvement through coaching and development to explaining the consequences of unchanging underperformance. Make your communication clear and straightforward. "This is the third time this has happened, and since your behavior hasn't changed, I need to explain the consequences." If you still don't see improvement after genuine efforts to boost your employee's performance, you may have to conclude that the person may not be the right fit for the organization.

Firing an employee is a painful process, but it may be the best choice for the organization and the rest of your team, which will only grow disheartened by working with an underperformer. Be sure to document progress (or lack thereof) along the way to guard against potential legal action, and consult with your legal and HR departments about how to best move forward with a dismissal.

Formal Performance Reviews

CHAPTER 12

The Case Against (and for) Annual Appraisals

Performance appraisal is a formal method for assessing how well an individual employee is doing with respect to established goals and expectations. These reviews have traditionally been conducted annually, though some organizations do offer them semiannually or quarterly, and they often include informal follow-ups as needed. Appraisal sessions are both a confirmation and a formalization of the ongoing feedback and development discussions that should be part of every manager-employee relationship.

Performance appraisals are not widely beloved, particularly by those being evaluated. In fact, they're probably the most stressful work conversation an employee will have all year. Even star performers may approach the review process with apprehension. Opening oneself to formal judgment—particularly judgment that can define one's pay—is rarely appealing.

But busy managers are not particularly fond of performance appraisals, either. They can be extremely time-consuming, requiring individualized preparation, administration, documentation, and follow-up that's tailored to each employee. For a manager with many direct reports, an appraisal for each person is a hefty time commitment. A study by corporate research and advisory firm CEB found that the average manager spends close to five weeks doing annual appraisals.[1] And managers find the process stressful as well: Few managers enjoy telling people that they're not doing their jobs as well as they should. "What a performance appraisal requires is for one person to stand in judgment of another," says Dick Grote, author of *How to Be Good at Performance Appraisals*. "Deep down, it's uncomfortable."[2]

But, done right, formal evaluations can help you reinforce solid work and redirect poor performance. At best, a review is an opportunity to reflect on performance and potential, allowing your direct report to improve in the future rather than be lambasted for past failures. When you consider that a manager's fundamental responsibility is to get results through their people, a systematic approach to assessing the work of one's direct reports seems a natural choice. In addition to providing insights into employee performance, appraisals help managers and organizations make informed, consistent decisions about pay, development, and promotions. Well-documented performance evaluations also protect the organization against lawsuits by employees who have been terminated, demoted, or denied a merit increase.

Your company may require you to do performance reviews annually, but that practice has come under question in the past few years, especially as it relates to performance ratings. If you have flexibility in your approach to formal assessments, you may want to take these criticisms into account.

The Argument Against Annual Appraisals

The historical focus of annual performance reviews was on determining which people to reward, keep, and terminate. The roots of traditional appraisals can be traced in large part back to two sources: the "merit rating" system developed in the U.S. military during World War I and Jack Welch's forced-ranking model used at GE, in which the top 10% of people were rewarded and the bottom 10% dismissed.

But as traditional performance management comes under fire, many organizations are concluding that formal performance reviews aren't delivering on their promises—that is, to improve employees' performance. When rapid innovation is a source of competitive advantage, a system geared toward assessing past performance doesn't help propel people forward.

Organizations are also increasingly questioning the accuracy of the evaluations themselves, particularly when it comes to ratings, where standardization simply cannot be achieved. Ratings are by nature subjective; two managers may mark the same person's skills differently, resulting in ratings that reveal more about the manager than the employee being evaluated. What's more, only an employee's "official" manager is tasked with appraising their performance—but that employee may be working on multiple teams or for several managers. It's unclear if one manager's point of view can account for the full range of an employee's performance. With an overemphasis on individual contribution, traditional appraisal systems fall short in accounting for or recognizing teamwork or collaboration—which are increasingly important.

Some difficulties with the review process also stem from the fact that appraisal conversations are used to discuss more than just performance. It's tough to have an open discussion about performance problems while also delivering news about merit pay. And appraisals, often intended as a bulwark against worst-case scenarios, are especially fraught when performance problems are significant. "Traditional corporate performance reviews are driven largely by fear of litigation," writes Patty McCord, former chief talent officer at Netflix, in her HBR article "How Netflix Reinvented HR." "The theory is that if you want to get rid of someone, you need a paper trail documenting a history of poor achievement." When these discussions only exist to ensure you're covered in case of a lawsuit, the emphasis on employee improvement is lost.

The annual gap between meetings also stilts the opportunity to elicit real change from your workers. A tired metaphor likens annual reviews to a yearly check-up with your doctor. The comparison isn't completely off base, but anyone who's ever visited an emergency room knows that one physical every 12 months does not equal sufficient health care. What if you have a medical condition that needs frequent monitoring, like asthma or even pregnancy? What if you sprain your ankle or get an infection? Waiting for your annual doctor's appointment won't cut it—and when it comes to performance, neither will an annual review.

Appraisals evaluate employees on how they have or haven't met goals set a year in advance. But when an organization can't foresee needs that far out, evaluating people on how they meet shorter-term goals and priorities can make more sense than assessing them in relation to annual goals. Organizations, particularly professional services and consulting firms, are also under increasing pressure to increase their learning and development efforts. When it comes to knowledge work, structured learning opportunities, including feedback and coaching, are what transforms green college graduates into skilled professionals. Meaningful feedback and coaching from managers is better delivered through frequent check-ins than in one annual conversation.

What's more, some employees *want* their performance reviewed more than once a year, particularly those (like Millennials) who are eager for constant learning and development, and making your employees wait a year to hear feedback leads to heightened anxiety when they sit down for the conversation. Employees shouldn't be surprised by a manager's appraisal—and if they are, they can become defensive or unwilling to hear the feedback. To continue producing good work, employees need more than a yearly dose of their supervisor's attention.

It's no surprise, then, that Wharton professor Peter Cappelli proclaims, "Performance appraisals are one of the most ubiquitous, and also one of the most unpopular, protocols in the workplace."[3] But if the traditional approach is fraught, what can managers—and organizations at large—do?

Alternate Approaches to Formal Reviews

It once seemed heretical to abandon traditional performance appraisal practices, but a growing number of companies are ditching performance evaluations while attempting to create new ways to more effectively manage performance. At least 30 of the *Fortune* 500 companies had revamped their performance appraisal practices by the end of 2015.[4]

Deloitte, for example, replaced its cumbersome evaluation and rating process with a streamlined new model: "something nimbler, real time, and more individualized —something squarely focused on fueling performance in the future rather than assessing it in the past," as Marcus Buckingham and Ashley Goodall describe in their HBR article, "Reinventing Performance Management." The consulting firm replaced their complex 360-degree feedback process with a quarterly "performance snapshot." Deloitte realized that while people may rate others' skills inconsistently, they are highly consistent when rating their own feelings and intentions. So, the company discovered, rather than asking more people about their opinion of an employee, they'd get a more effective response by asking the individual's immediate team leader four key questions that focus on what they'd *do* with the individual, rather than what they *think* of them. This forward-thinking questionnaire focused on four areas: compensation, teamwork, poor performance, and promotion. Complementing the quarterly snapshot are frequent weekly check-ins.

Netflix, too, eliminated formal performance reviews, stating that they were "too ritualistic and too infrequent." They encourage regular conversations between managers and employees, but the company also implemented informal, simple 360-degree reviews that asked people to identify things their colleagues should stop, start, or continue doing. Netflix began by using a software program to elicit responses but has since shifted to signed feedback or even face-to-face conversations. According to McCord, "If you talk simply and honestly about performance on a regular basis, you can get good results— probably better ones than a company that grades everyone on a five-point scale."

Other companies choose to keep their annual appraisals but make changes to the actual event. For example, Facebook analyzed its performance management system and found that 87% of people wanted to keep performance ratings.[5] So they kept their annual reviews but revised their rating process to improve fairness and transparency and to increase their focus on development.

GE, originator of much of the traditional appraisal process, is working to replace its legacy system with a real-time approach in which managers and their employees hold frequent, informal "touchpoint" conversations to set or update priorities based on customer needs. But these forward-looking, ongoing discussions are complemented with a year-end summary conversation and document (not unlike the traditional annual review), during which both manager and employee reflect on impact achieved and look ahead. Managers base compensation, promotion, and development decisions on these summary findings—just as they did under GE's previous system. With the company's new "performance development" approach, however, the manager and employee have a richer set of data concerning the employee's contributions and impact over the course of the year, so the end-of-year discussions are both more future focused and more meaningful.[6]

Companies are also rethinking the use of time-consuming, set systems and processes in favor of allowing managers more leeway in evaluating employees. Letting people rely on logic and common sense can lead to better results than adhering to inflexible formal policies, and newer evaluation approaches generally require more discussion and less documentation, making them less cumbersome and formal, more agile and flexible.

These organizations, though, represent just a small portion of companies that are changing the way they're looking at formal appraisals. Traditional annual reviews are still widely used. According to a study by *Human Resource Executive*, "Despite all the buzz about abolishing formal performance reviews, the vast majority of organizations continue to employ traditional vehicles for sharing performance-related information."[7] In part, that's because employees do need to be evaluated. Performance inevitably must be measured and rated—and if the appraisal process is eliminated, those evaluations will be invisible to employees. Managers may draw conclusions about a direct report's performance, but without the opportunity to get input from the employee. And without rankings or numerical measures, it can be difficult to tie financial rewards to performance in a standardized way.

If organizations dismiss annual appraisals, they need to replace them with something, whether that means more-frequent formal reviews—semiannual or quarterly —or informal periodic check-in conversations.

Performance Reviews Moving Forward

So what does this mean for you as a manager? Unless you're the CEO, it's unlikely you can overhaul your entire organization's approach to appraisal, but you can control the way you manage the performance of your team. If your organization requires reviews—whether they are annual, semiannual, or quarterly—you should, of course, do them. But you can take additional steps throughout the review period to ensure that your employees are meeting goals and growing with the organization.

Make a practice of checking in with each of your direct reports on a weekly basis—or at least once a month—to ask two main questions: What are you going to get done this week (or month)? And what help do you need from me? These informal conversations don't require complex forms or burdensome documentation. Check-ins like these are your best opportunity to deliver immediate, relevant feedback—and real-time, in-the-moment course correction.

When you are faced with conducting periodic formal reviews, there are proven ways to make them easier for you and more effective for your employees—a topic that we'll explore in the coming chapters.

NOTES

1. "The Real Impact of Eliminating Performance Ratings: Insights from Employees and Managers," CEB Global, 2016.

2. Quoted in Rebecca Knight, "Delivering an Effective Performance Review," HBR.org, November 3, 2011, https://hbr.org/2011/11/delivering-an-effective-perfor.

3. Peter Cappelli, "The Common Myths About Performance Reviews, Debunked," HBR.org, July 26, 2016 (product #H030NZ).

4. Lori Goler, Janelle Gale, and Adam Grant, "Let's Not Kill Performance Evaluations Yet," *Harvard Business Review*, November 2016 (product #R1611G).

5. Ibid.

6. Peter Cappelli and Anna Tavis, "The Performance Management Revolution," *Harvard Business Review*, October 2016 (product #R1610D).

7. "Seeking Agility in Performance Management," *Human Resource Executive*, http://hr1.silkroad.com/hr-exec-agility-performance-management.

CHAPTER 13

Assess Performance, but Rethink Ratings

There is no one right way to conduct a performance appraisal, but you and your direct report will both benefit from your preparation. You must evaluate your direct report's performance in relation to the goals you defined together. You can use the same methods described in section 2 to identify gaps between goals and performance.

You'll also want to assess behaviors that may not be explicitly linked to any specific goal. Teamwork, communication skills, leadership, initiative, focus, productivity, and reliability are all competencies that affect how an employee gets work done. You may also want to consider whether or not someone has demonstrated citizenship behaviors, like helping their colleagues or making new hires feel welcome, which boost cooperation and improve the work environment.

Gather Information About Performance

Appraisals are too easily skewed by a manager's limited perspective and selective memory. One big mistake or contribution over the course of the review period may stick in a manager's mind and outweigh everything else their direct report has done during that time. And because an employee's most recent performance is fresh in their manager's mind, that behavior can weigh more heavily in the evaluation than it should. But you can help avoid these problems by drawing on different sources of information to get a fuller picture.

There are a number of resources to take under consideration when evaluating performance. If you've been keeping records on your ongoing feedback, coaching, and development conversations, you'll have plenty of material to work with. You can also gather 360-degree feedback from others to complement your own observations. But to begin, you want to solicit your employee's point of view.

Request an employee's self-assessment

About two weeks before the review session, ask your direct report to complete a self-evaluation. This document allows you to take the employee's input into account when you're preparing for the conversation, rather than potentially being surprised by it just before or during the formal review. Such self-appraisal also has the benefit of setting a tone of partnership that may help the person be more open to subsequent feedback.

Some organizations provide specific self-evaluation forms or checklists. Questions on this form may include:

- What are your most important accomplishments since your last review?

- Have you achieved the goals set for this review period?

- Have you surpassed any of your goals? Which ones? What helped you exceed them?

- Are you currently struggling with any goals? Which ones? What is inhibiting your progress toward those goals (lack of training, inadequate resources, poor direction from management)?

- Has this review period been better or worse than previous ones in the position?

- What parts of your job do you find most and least interesting or enjoyable?

- What do you most like and dislike about working for this organization?

- What do you consider to be your most important tasks and aims for the upcoming year?

- What can I as your manager, or the organization as a whole, do to help you be more successful?

Answering these questions can enhance your employee's ability to learn and reflect during your appraisal discussion. The very act of thinking them over will help the individual recognize the review not as a required drill but as a true effort toward helping them understand how they're contributing to the organization and how they might build success.

Even if you aren't required to use a formal self-appraisal form, it's still worth soliciting some information from your direct report. Ask for an informal list of your direct report's most important achievements and accomplishments—projects, tasks, relevant initiatives—over the review period to ensure you don't overlook any of your employee's successes. This can be as simple as an email with bullet points. You can also ask them for a list of people you could check with about their performance (the 360-degree feedback process). This input can give you a broader perspective on the employee's work and any related problems, since as a manager you may be seeing just a small part of what the person does or struggles with every day. It will also help refresh your memory and put a positive slant on an event that so many participants dread.

Some argue that self-appraisals don't work. For example, performance evaluation expert Dick Grote says that self-assessments give the employee the wrong impression of what an appraisal is, not to mention a false sense of collaboration, especially if someone's performance is unacceptable. Having a direct report complete a self-appraisal cues them to expect that they'll bring their evaluation, you'll bring yours, and together you'll come to an agreement on the final appraisal. But a performance evaluation is a record of your opinion of the quality of their work—not a negotiation.

In cases where there may be confusion—for example, an underperformer's work is unacceptable and requires immediate change—you may choose not to solicit a self-assessment. But if you do use self-appraisals in the review process, make it clear to your direct report that their contribution is just one piece of the data that you'll review when looking at the whole picture and that its purpose is for you to gain insight into their point of view.

Review your records

In addition to the employee's self-assessment, read over any notes you've kept on your direct report over the review period. If you've kept robust records, you won't need to rack your brain trying to remember what happened over the course of the year; you'll have the information right in front of you.

If you're preparing for a review and don't have detailed records, consider what sources you do have to jog your memory. Skim through your calendar appointments to remind yourself of specific accomplishments or problems—the sales pitch delivered flawlessly, the deadline missed, or the time your employee smoothly covered for a colleague during flu season. Look through email correspondence and meeting notes to find similar details that may have escaped you.

Solicit 360-degree feedback

You may also want to consider complementing your own observations with 360-degree feedback: feedback from colleagues and others who work closely with your direct report. For instance, an "internal customer"—someone for whom your employee provides, say, tech or design services—and a peer who works with the employee on a cross-functional team might have valuable input on dimensions of the person's work that you don't see directly. Gaining observations from the employee's larger community can expand your limited perspective.

This type of broad feedback that synthesizes others' perspectives can reduce the chance of a performance misdiagnosis. It also recognizes that many modern workplaces are multifaceted, with no one person in particular seeing all dimensions of the employee's work. Thus, several people in a position to know are asked to rate the quality of the subject's performance and their interactions with them. Some organizations present this feedback anonymously; others have colleagues participate in direct conversations about one another's work.

As a method, 360-degree feedback is not without drawbacks. First, it is time-consuming. Think for a moment about the many people whom you might be asked to rate in your organization. Your boss, four or five of your peers, the person who handles your department's expense reimbursements, and so forth. Now multiply that number by the one hour typically required to prepare an evaluation. This time adds up.

People can also be uncomfortable giving a negative report about someone else—even when that person has glaring shortcomings or you assure them their responses will remain anonymous. The reviewers know that their report might result in no raise for (or even dismissal of) their colleague. But within an organization that's committed to providing useful feedback and in which people understand the value of the 360-degree approach, soliciting others' points of view can provide much more complete information on a direct report's work than you, as an individual, possibly can. On the other hand, if an employee works with very few people or if asking for such feedback would not fit within your organization's culture, 360-degree feedback may not add much to your own evaluation.

Your organization may have a set process for facilitating 360-degree feedback, but if it doesn't, consider these tips for getting the most-useful information:

- **Diversify your pool of respondents.** Tap a number of peers, direct reports, and internal and external customers to provide input, rather than asking people from only one category or just one person from each category. Inviting a larger pool of participants means you'll get a more complete picture, the respondents will feel more comfortable sharing their feedback knowing they're not a lone identifiable voice, and your employee will be assured that you've worked to gather a broad, balanced view.

- **Clarify that your purpose is constructive, not punitive.** Explain to all involved—those giving feedback and those receiving it—that the purpose of the 360 review isn't to amass criticism but to evaluate achievements and define areas for improvement.

- **Request specific examples rather than just numeric ratings.** If you're asking about communication skills, you'll learn much more from a response like "José answers all my questions clearly and patiently" than you will from a 5 out of 5 rating in communication.

- **Ask probing questions.** Dig deeper into people's responses by asking thoughtful questions such as, How did this person contribute? What do you want this person to stop, start, and continue doing? What are their strengths as a collaborator, and what are their weaknesses?

Find additional information

Between your employee's self-assessment, your own records, and the feedback of others, you should already be forming an objective picture of an individual's performance. But consider other resources when assessing your employee's work as well, including:

- The employee's job description. You're not just evaluating the quality of your employee's work but determining how well they performed their specific job function.

- The person's goals and development plan as defined in the last review or during the review period. When assessing performance against goals, it's helpful to revisit those goals—taking into account any that may have changed over the course of the review period—to see if they've been successfully completed.

- Any documents from previous review sessions, prior evaluation forms, employment records, and other relevant material you may have on file.

After gathering your information, the next step is to pull it together into an overarching evaluation you'll later share with your employee.

Assess Performance

To synthesize the information you've gathered, sift through it and begin noting common themes. Look for patterns and recurring threads, and just as you did when preparing to give feedback, focus on things that, if addressed, will make a difference in future performance. There's no reason to rehash a onetime mistake, like the botched presentation six months ago that the employee underprepared for and that you've already discussed with them. On the other hand, if they've consistently presented poorly, and they're still not sufficiently preparing despite multiple feedback discussions, you would be wise to address it in your formal appraisal.

Give equal consideration to positive results and to shortcomings when analyzing the overall picture. Has your direct report met the goals set for the review period? (It could be that their goals have changed since you initially set them a year ago, so take that into account.) It's easiest to evaluate quantitative achievements—such as the numbers of presentations delivered, reports written, or apps developed—but to assess qualitative aspects of their work, focus on behaviors and supplement your evaluation with examples.

It can be difficult to assess performance against goals. Sure, if the goal is to assemble 150 widgets or generate mortgage loans equal to $3.5 million, it's simple to make an accurate calculation. But few jobs are that clear-cut. What if measuring someone's "output" requires evaluating how well they managed a team, influenced others, or helped people collaborate? In cases like these, assessment is more subjective. As a manager, you see only part of the employee's work activity over the course of the year. The 360-degree feedback you collected will be especially helpful in assessing how they're regarded by others and in gauging the scope and quality of their influence.

As you sift through your data, also consider how the employee has performed against behavioral expectations. Communication skills, for example, are critical for someone in a customer service role, just as coding skills are vital for a developer. Focus in on those behaviors that are most important for an employee's success in their particular role. (Looking back at the job description or competency model for the position or level in the organization can help here.) Your organization may want you to focus on key behaviors or competencies or on how company values were demonstrated. Also take into account more-general attributes like initiative, cooperation and teamwork, efficiency, dependability, and improvement that may not be specific to the role or organization.

As you begin to draw conclusions about an employee's performance, remember context. An individual's performance depends, to varying degrees, on the situation in which they work. It's not always fair or accurate to evaluate two colleagues in the same position on the same criteria, using the same scale or inflexible reference points. Consider situational factors in a call center, for example, where performance is assessed based on the dollar amount of charitable donations pledged. Different results can be caused by differences in the geographic regions or the populations of potential donors the employees are assigned. Such underlying factors may affect your direct report's performance. It's worth considering questions such as:

- What situational factors made it easier or harder for this person to achieve their goals?

- What systems, processes, structures, circumstances, or events helped or hindered this employee's performance?

- How have I contributed to this employee's success or performance problems?

Documenting the Performance Evaluation

In many organizations, you'll be required to document your impressions and feedback in a way that can be shared and saved. Your company may already have a set of questions to answer or a standard form to use. If not, you can create your own by adapting the performance evaluation form template in table 13-1 at the end of this chapter.

Record your observations about your employee's job performance as objectively as possible, and support them with examples. Provide evidence of progress (or lack thereof) by connecting accomplishments with established goals. For example: "Derek increased sales by 12%, which exceeded his goal of 10%." "Amelia reduced her error rate by 18%; her goal was 25%." Including the background data informing your conclusions will help your direct report grasp the assessment criteria and recognize the evaluation as fair.

Your organization may require you to provide ratings—a general ranking of the employee's performance or individual ratings of specific aspects of their performance. But a numeric value alone may not give your employee enough information to make improvements or continue good work. Instead, supplement your rating with qualitative examples, written and verbal observations, and comments that explain your choices. (See the sidebar "Navigating Ratings.")

NAVIGATING RATINGS

Ratings used to be an established part of many organization's performance appraisal processes. Despite movements away from this step, some organizations still require that managers rate or score their employees annually on a 5- (or sometimes 3- or 4-) point scale. And some of these require forced rankings, in which only 1 or 2 of 10 people can get the highest rating.

Some companies still find the process of rating valuable. At Facebook, for example, managers deliberate over those ratings in groups, to keep individual employees from being unduly punished or rewarded by managers who are hard or easy "graders." Ratings are also used when making decisions about compensation.

But just as performance reviews are changing, so too is the practice of using performance ratings. Companies are discovering that ratings aren't as effective as they hoped they'd be. For instance, in his HBR article "Performance Appraisal Reappraised," Dick Grote described a workplace where nearly all annual ratings of 3,200 employees were positive. Not one person was rated "unsatisfactory"; just one had been deemed "marginal." "Clearly, such uniformly glowing appraisals are useless in evaluating the relative merits of staff members," Grote writes. The result is general "performance inflation" in which nearly everyone is rated above average—a statistical impossibility.

Ratings may no longer make sense in a changing work context. Many people work in teams that their direct managers may not observe, doing cross-functional work their managers may not even understand, let alone be able to assess accurately, so an immediate manager's rating may not be correct or meaningful. As more people work in teams and as

(continued)

NAVIGATING RATINGS

collaboration is increasingly valued, the traditional-forced rankingapproach also leads to competition, reducing the likelihood of open collaboration and damaging overall team-based performance. In response to these arguments, more and more organizations are ditching the use of ratings and forced distribution.

If you are required to rate your direct report, certainly do as your organization dictates, but keep in mind a few caveats. A five-point scale is not analogous to A–F grades in a school context. The majority of employees will get a 3, the middle rank. Some individuals may be disappointed with a 3 rating, thinking they're merely average. In this context, a 3 means someone has hit their goal targets with solid, satisfactory performance. "In school, a C was mediocre," Grote explains, "but a 3 in the working world means they're meeting expectations. They're shooting par."[1]

In addition, combine your rating with specific comments and feedback that give the employee a clear understanding of why they got their rating and how their performance is aligning with their goals. If there isn't space on your organization's evaluation form, add a page to allow yourself room to explain the logic behind the rating, and discuss your rating during the meeting itself as well. Your employee will find your comments, observations, and qualitative examples valuable complements to a static quantitative score.

The more specific information you can provide to back up your conclusions, the more likely the employee will be to repeat and even improve on positive behaviors—and to correct negative ones. Use the most-telling examples to make your point in your written evaluation, and save the rest for your review session in case you need to support your judgment during the conversation. Examples should include:

- **Details about what you observed.** For instance, Theo, a customer service representative, has more than doubled the orders he's filled over the past year now that he's learned how to use a new customer database. Back that assessment up with detail in your write-up: "Last year Theo filled 15 orders per day. This year his average exceeded 30 per day. He also asks fewer questions now that he's effectively using the customer database."

- **Supporting data, perhaps from 360-degree feedback.** "Siobhan helped Theo learn how to use the new customer database, and she reports that he's using it on a regular basis."

- **The impact on your team and organization.** "After Theo learned how to use the new database, he no longer had to rely on colleagues to find out pertinent information. The whole team began fulfilling orders more quickly because they were answering fewer questions from him, which improved cash flow for the organization."

Expressing your observations as neutral facts rather than judgments is particularly important when it concerns subpar results. "Theo received five complaints from extremely unsatisfied customers" is objective, non-judgmental, and specific to a particular job requirement. Contrast that with a negative characterization that doesn't describe actual behavior ("Theo doesn't seem to care about customers") or a vague judgment that fails to point to a specific skill he might improve ("Theo doesn't know how to talk to difficult customers").

When giving positive feedback, on the other hand, combine specific achievements with character-based praise. For example: "With the new accounts she generated, which delivered $1.25 million in business, Juliana exceeded the goal we set for her last July by 27%. Her creativity and perseverance drove her to look beyond the traditional client base; she researched new industries and networked at conferences to find new customers." Acknowledging the traits and behaviors that made those results possible will show your direct report that you see them as an individual and recognize their unique contributions. Such praise can generate pride and boost motivation in your employee.

Supporting your assessment with specific examples, data, and details increases the likelihood that the employee will be able to absorb and learn from your feedback, and it also mitigates any possible legal ramifications in particularly egregious situations. If a person's work is beginning to suffer, or if you suspect that you might need to dismiss someone due to poor performance, it's vital that you document the individual's behavior and the steps you've taken to correct it. As a rule of thumb, include in your evaluation only statements that you'd be comfortable testifying to in court. If you have any questions about legal ramifications, consult with your human resource manager or internal legal team.

Finally, write down the three things the employee has done best over the course of the year and the two areas that most need improvement. Distill your message down to one key idea—your overall impression of their performance, which is the single most important takeaway for your direct report. These few points will determine the overarching message that you want to convey in the review discussion, and having them documented will prevent you from forgetting any important details when you're in the conversation.

NOTE

1. Quoted in Rebecca Knight, "Delivering an Effective Performance Review," HBR.org, November 3, 2011, https://hbr.org/2011/11/delivering-an-effective-perfor.

TABLE 13-1

Performance evaluation form template

Employee information	
Review period	
Employee	
Job title	
Department	
Manager	

Scale for competencies	
Exemplary	Performance far exceeds the expectations of the position.
Excellent	Performance exceeds the expectations of the position.
Satisfactory	Performance fully meets the expectations of the position.
Fair	Performance does not meet the expectations of the position and requires some improvement.
Unsatisfactory	Performance is far below the expectations of the position and requires significant improvement.

Key accomplishments

Goals

Was each goal met?

Goal 1	Goal 2	Goal 3
☐ Yes ☐ No	☐ Yes ☐ No	☐ Yes ☐ No

Competencies: Rate the employee on all relevant competencies.

Job requirements: Fulfills required responsibilities for position
☐ Exemplary ☐ Excellent ☐ Satisfactory ☐ Fair ☐ Unsatisfactory
Comments:

Problem solving: Demonstrates ability to solve problems and execute solutions
☐ Exemplary ☐ Excellent ☐ Satisfactory ☐ Fair ☐ Unsatisfactory
Comments:

Initiative: Demonstrates ambition to succeed in the position and strives to improve processes and products
☐ Exemplary ☐ Excellent ☐ Satisfactory ☐ Fair ☐ Unsatisfactory
Comments:

Efficiency: Completes assigned tasks on time without wasting time or resources
☐ Exemplary ☐ Excellent ☐ Satisfactory ☐ Fair ☐ Unsatisfactory
Comments:

Teamwork: Works well with others and contributes to group projects
☐ Exemplary ☐ Excellent ☐ Satisfactory ☐ Fair ☐ Unsatisfactory
Comments:

Communication: Writes and speaks with clarity; interacts effectively with managers, peers, or customers
☐ Exemplary ☐ Excellent ☐ Satisfactory ☐ Fair ☐ Unsatisfactory
Comments:

Adaptability: Is receptive to new ideas or change within the team or business and makes adjustments to work as necessary
☐ Exemplary ☐ Excellent ☐ Satisfactory ☐ Fair ☐ Unsatisfactory
Comments:

(continued)

Formal Performance Reviews

TABLE 13-1 (*continued*)

Leadership: Demonstrates ability to influence or lead others toward achieving unit, team, or firm goals
☐ Exemplary ☐ Excellent ☐ Satisfactory ☐ Fair ☐ Unsatisfactory
Comments:

Integrity: Is honest and fair and models organizational values
☐ Exemplary ☐ Excellent ☐ Satisfactory ☐ Fair ☐ Unsatisfactory
Comments:

Accountability: Accepts responsibility for failure or errors
☐ Exemplary ☐ Excellent ☐ Satisfactory ☐ Fair ☐ Unsatisfactory
Comments:

Judgment: Makes sound choices and informed decisions; able to distinguish between issues that need immediate attention and those that can wait
☐ Exemplary ☐ Excellent ☐ Satisfactory ☐ Fair ☐ Unsatisfactory
Comments:

Dependability: Elicits trust from colleagues; delivers consistently on promises and commitments
☐ Exemplary ☐ Excellent ☐ Satisfactory ☐ Fair ☐ Unsatisfactory
Comments:

Improvement: Demonstrates improved performance over the review period
☐ Exemplary ☐ Excellent ☐ Satisfactory ☐ Fair ☐ Unsatisfactory
Comments:

Areas of strength for the employee

Areas of development for the employee

Additional comments

Signatures

Manager signature and date:

Signature   Date

To be signed by the employee after receipt of the performance evaluation form and discussion with the employee's manager.

Employee signature and date:

Signature   Date

Source: Adapted from *HBR Guide to Delivering Effective Feedback Ebook + Tools* (Boston: Harvard Business Review Press, 2016), product #10084E.

CHAPTER 14

How to Conduct the Review Conversation

The detailed information you've captured in your performance evaluation form is a helpful guide for when you sit down with your individual team members. But simply stating what is on paper won't convince your employee to change or motivate them to continue their good work. You need to give just as much careful consideration to the discussion itself.

Much like with your ongoing feedback discussions, the logistics around your performance appraisal meeting are just as important as the points you want to communicate. Without establishing the right time, place, and tone, your message may be lost, and your direct report may not understand what to do next.

Even star performers may feel some anxiety at the prospect of a formal review conversation, so do what you can to put your employee at ease. Then, launch into a two-way discussion about performance.

Consider Logistics

Schedule the performance review session well in advance to give both of you the opportunity to prepare, and be thoughtful about choosing a meeting time. Don't infringe on personal time by proposing a meeting during lunch or after work. Set aside 45 to 60 minutes for your conversation, and make sure that neither of you has a pressing commitment immediately afterward in case the discussion takes longer than expected or your direct report needs some time to work through any emotions brought on by what might be a difficult conversation. You may want to ask when they would prefer to meet—a subtle signal that you value their time.

Choose a location that will make your employee feel comfortable, somewhere private and free from distractions and interruptions. You'll both be most at ease in a business setting—an empty office, a conference room—rather than in a cafeteria, coffee shop, or restaurant. Try to find a neutral spot, but if you do meet in your office, sit beside the person to establish a sense of partnership and open communication. Sitting behind your desk, especially in the context of delivering a judgment, can convey dominance and distance.

Explain the nature of the meeting ahead of time, even if the two of you have had review sessions in the past. Outline what you plan to discuss, which may include the employee's input or self-assessment, your completed evaluation, a rating (should your organization require it), a summary of their strengths, and areas for improvement. In most cases, you'll want to give your direct report a copy of your appraisal about an hour or so before you meet and ask them to note any questions or comments. Allow them some privacy to read the document over carefully. "When people read someone's assessment of them, they are going to have all sorts of churning emotions," says performance evaluation expert Dick Grote. "Let them have that on their own time, and give them a chance to think about it."[1]

Some employees may require special arrangements, especially if the discussion has the possibility of escalating to an uncomfortable level. For an individual whose work is unacceptable, for instance, schedule a time to meet near the end of the day, and plan to meet in your office. You may also choose not to provide your employee with their completed evaluation in advance of the meeting. These small changes will place you in a position of authority, indicate the need for improvement, and allow the employee to decompress afterward if they have an emotional reaction to the feedback.

Set the Correct Tone

To mitigate any anxiety and establish rapport, set a tone of partnership right from the start. Welcome your employee, try to put them at ease, and limit distractions. Close the door, and silence any notifications on your phone or computer. You should have already established a relationship of trust through your discussions throughout the review period, but if not, taking clear steps to demonstrate your respect for your direct report in this conversation can help. Active listening is key to making your employee feel truly heard. Resist the temptation to check your watch or your phone during the course of the conversation.

Remind the employee of the meeting's purpose: to determine how well the individual is doing with respect to assigned goals and to motivate good performance, provide constructive feedback, and understand more about what they need to do to excel in their job. Tell them explicitly that their input is necessary and valuable and that you hope the conversation will be an open dialogue so you can work together on any issues that arise. You should also mention that you'd like to take notes so that you can both remember what you've discussed.

Once you've clarified the meeting's purpose and objectives, ask questions to help you understand the employee's perspective on their performance and to keep you from controlling too much of the conversation early on. If they seem reluctant to speak up, you might probe with questions like, "How do you feel things are going on the job? What's going well, and what problems are you having?" or "Tell me some of the main points you want me to note from your self-evaluation." Focus on their point of view rather than agreeing or disagreeing.

As you would in any important conversation, practice active listening. Don't interrupt. Show that you're paying close attention by periodically paraphrasing what you've heard. You might say, "If I understand you correctly, you feel that you are meeting all goals with respect to the weekly sales reports but that you are struggling to contact all the key customers you've been assigned. Do I have that right?" This gives your direct report the opportunity to correct any misunderstandings.

It's not uncommon for an employee to request a pay increase or inquire about a promotion during appraisal discussions. These topics should not be the focus of your conversation, but if you're asked directly, be prepared to respond. The sidebar "When an Employee Asks for a Raise or Promotion" explains how to tackle these requests.

WHEN AN EMPLOYEE ASKS FOR A RAISE OR PROMOTION

Many people ask for a change in pay or title in the context of performance review meetings. If possible, keep this discussion of compensation separate by holding it at a later date. Performance and compensation are each significant enough on their own to warrant dedicated conversations, and it's seldom ideal to mix the two. Thank your direct report for bringing up the topic and promise to get back to them by a specific date. (If it's already been decided whether a raise or promotion will be granted, however, and the individual is set on discussing it as part of your review meeting, do so at the beginning of your conversation; otherwise your employee may be too distracted to take in your feedback.)

(continued)

WHEN AN EMPLOYEE ASKS FOR A RAISE OR PROMOTION

If your direct report is asking for an increase in pay and a decision about salary hasn't yet been made, you'll need time to fairly assess the situation and determine whether a pay increase is appropriate. And even if you think a pay increase is merited, don't grant it immediately. Word will get out that all a person needs to get a raise is to ask.

When you do meet again to discuss the request, explain that an individual's salary is determined by two factors: the value of the job itself to the organization and the quality of the individual's performance. In some cases, you may discover that someone is well deserving, but there's no opportunity for an increase in compensation. Regardless of the individual in the role, every job is worth a certain market value. If that position's pay isn't negotiable because it has reached the peak compensation your organization allows for that role, tell your employee so: Rejecting a raise request in that situation will clearly reflect only the value of the job to the organization, not the person's worth as an individual.

In other instances, your employee may be more interested in a change in title than in a raise alone. In such cases you'll need to assess their ability to take on the new job (and if that position is feasible in the organization). You may decide that your direct report isn't quite ready to take the next step. In that event, focus on what they can do to get to the next level. Joseph Weintraub, author of *The Coaching Manager*, suggests saying something along the lines of, "You're not ready today. This next level has a different set of criteria and skills. But let's talk about how you're going to get there."[2]

You'll have to explain what skills, knowledge, and experience your employee will need before a promotion is possible and assure them that you're committed to helping them succeed. Work with them to identify the gaps between their current skills and experience and where they need to be in order to step into the new role they desire. Strategize ways to fill those gaps using some of the development tactics discussed in chapter 9, including enriching and challenging stretch assignments, training, or mentoring.

Discuss Performance

Managers can feel nervous, even reluctant, about offering constructive feedback in the review session. But everyone, even your best performers, can benefit from hearing ideas for improvement—and missing out on this opportunity to deliver feedback means your time-consuming evaluation won't be of much use.

Tailor your discussion to each employee you're meeting with, and don't rely on your written assessment to dictate the agenda. Adhering to the order of an inflexible form can lock you and your direct report into an item-by-item negotiation instead of a productive discussion. Instead, use your evaluation as a reference so you remember to cover all the important points you planned to mention.

The employee's performance—not the employee themselves—should be the subject of the conversation. Focus your discussion on how agreed-upon performance goals relate to specific outcomes. For example, "We agreed that you'd bring in 10 new clients this quarter, and you exceeded that goal" or "We agreed that you'd reduce the number of production line errors by 10%, but you've only reduced them by 5%." Emphasize issues that the person can improve in the future. Be selective; you don't need to go over every shortcoming or failing you've noticed, only the most important ones.

As in your written evaluation, don't make any statements about your direct report's character, values, or intentions. Doing so can make your employee defensive and is unlikely to lead to fruitful ideas for change or improvement. Instead, use neutral language like, "I've noticed you haven't offered any suggestions at our service improvement meetings. Why is that?" Take care not to express any anger, judgment, or contempt, even with employees whose performance needs significant improvement.

Avoid any use of the stale "sandwich" technique (as discussed in chapter 5), in which you share some praise, then deliver criticism, and end with more positive feedback. It can be tempting to sugarcoat constructive comments, but couching your tough feedback in fluffy compliments will only distort what you're trying to communicate, making it less likely that your direct report will discern your real message and make needed adjustments. With the sandwich approach, you can unwittingly dishearten your best employees and misguide your poorest ones.

For most of your employees—your good, solid performers and your exceptional ones—you should focus your discussion on their successes. Highlighting what competent contributors are doing well can further motivate them. For marginal performers, you'll need to take a different approach.

Recognizing strong performance

For those employees whose results and behaviors fully meet or exceed expectations, concentrate on strengths by recognizing and celebrating what they've done well. Thank your employee for their contributions. They may not know how much you appreciate their good work. This will grab their attention and also reduce the defensiveness that they might have felt at the prospect of a performance review.

Detail specific examples where their successes and strengths were most apparent: "You've increased our social media following by 8%, you did a terrific job in organizing the quarterly marketing meetings, and your contributions at staff meetings are exemplary." By starting with their most important contributions and most noteworthy strengths, focusing on achievements and pinpointing the behaviors that led to success, you'll encourage your direct report's drive and motivation.

For star performers, introduce improvements within the context of their strengths and contributions. Your conscientious employee will likely acknowledge any missed targets or unmet goals and may initiate a discussion of opportunities for improvement. If so, they can take the lead in discussing opportunities for development, which will allow them to be more invested in the conversation and "own" improvement efforts.

If your employee doesn't volunteer any areas for change, prompt them with questions such as, How do you see the situation? What do you think worked, and what could have gone better? How might you do things differently in the future? By asking questions rather than making statements, you can establish a supportive atmosphere without devaluing any of their accomplishments. By answering your questions, the person can raise issues and explore alternative approaches.

Discussing areas for improvement (however minor) may naturally lead you to talk about development opportunities. You can also delve into achievements, both to keep the person on their successful course and to find out if the employee has learned something that can benefit others. Ask, "How did you manage to do that so well?" Identifying what made the person successful can open the topic of career aspirations and avenues for further development.

Conducting appraisals for marginal performers

Performance evaluations for employees who require serious improvement should be held last. You might be tempted to get a potentially unpleasant conversation out of the way, but your skill at conducting a review session will improve with practice. You'll gain experience with easier appraisals (with your stars, for example) before you tackle this tough conversation.

If an employee's performance—their work results, behaviors, or a combination of both—is subpar, the focus of the review session should be on immediate turnaround in order for the individual to remain employed. Open the conversation by reminding the employee of the purpose of the review and acknowledging that this sort of meeting can feel awkward. Then get right to the point: "I need to tell you that your performance is not acceptable. I want to spend our time together talking about the problems I see and hearing your ideas about what you can do to correct this situation."

After this blunt opening, explain clearly what problems you perceive and make it clear that these issues must be fixed. This three-step approach can be useful:

- **State your concern precisely:** "Your approach to customer service is of serious concern."

- **Follow with examples:** "Some customers have complained about your sarcastic and condescending tone. They've noted you seem impatient and have referred to their questions as 'dumb.'"

- **Close by requesting the employee's reaction to your perception or with a specific request for change:** "I need you to change your customer service style. If you're not willing to do that, then customer service might not be the right career for you."

This direct confrontation of unacceptable performance will be painful for the employee to hear. Marginal performers may be used to the old sandwich technique, which enabled them to selectively focus on the few positive comments and brush off any discussion of problems. They may be surprised by your negative, one-sided approach, perhaps responding that previous years' reviews have always been good and that their work this year was no different. You might acknowledge that the employee has been done a disservice by not having the facts presented clearly in previous reviews, but that doesn't change the fact that their performance this year was not acceptable, and immediate correction must occur if they are to remain employed.

As a manager, you may find this approach uncomfortable; most of us dislike confrontation. But excessive diplomacy can be just as damaging as undue harshness. Employees can't adjust their behavior in a meaningful way if the criticism they hear is indirect or sugarcoated. Embrace an opportunity to deliver and discuss meaningful criticism. Every employee deserves an honest assessment.

Some poor performers, however, may honestly believe their work has been satisfactory. In this case, frankly correct the misconception, and give the employee an opportunity to improve. The individual's performance may get substantially better with direction and support. If not, you may determine that the person is better suited to a lower-level position or that they might not be the right fit for the organization.

Get It on the Record

Documenting the details of the review session will benefit both you and your employee in case of disagreement over what you discussed or planned during the review (and in the rarer case of legal disputes). So during your conversation, jot down the main points. Include the following information in your notes:

- The date of the meeting

- Who attended (in some cases, your boss or a human resource representative may attend)

- Key points and phrases the employee used (not necessarily verbatim)

- Any points of disagreement

Take notes with pen and paper; a computer screen can create distraction and distance between the two of you. Type up your notes right after the meeting, while your memory is still fresh.

Your organization may require you to distribute copies of this record to the employee and to HR for the employee's file. You should keep a copy as well. Some organizations request that both manager and employee sign the performance review report, and sometimes the employee has the right to append their own comments.

It's helpful to separate the review and development or performance-planning sessions over time. Review conversations and constructive criticism can rouse strong feelings, and it can be difficult to engage an emotional person in creating a plan for future development or in nailing down a new set of goals. If you are able, separate the meetings by a week or so, and let your employee know at the review session that today you'll discuss performance, and next week you'll follow up to talk about plans for development or goal setting. This gives them time to process your feedback and mull over ways they can improve and grow.

That said, if any potential goals or development opportunities do arise in your review sessions, you'll want to note those as well. Write down any performance goals for the coming year, an overview of any development plans you and your direct report talk about, and a summary of agreed-upon next steps, so you'll have it for any future discussions.

NOTES

1. Quoted in Rebecca Knight, "Delivering an Effective Performance Review," HBR.org, November 3, 2011, https://hbr.org/2011/11/delivering-an-effective-perfor.
2. Quoted in Rebecca Knight, "What to Do When Your Employee Asks for a Raise Too Soon," HBR.org, July 15, 2016 (product #H030GB).

CHAPTER 15

Define New Goals for a New Cycle

Performance management is an ongoing and continuous process, so the appraisal conversation should not serve as a hard stop. Start the cycle anew by following up with your employee for a performance-planning session after the appraisal to discuss the new goals they'll start working toward, and embrace the opportunity to evaluate your own approach to performance management by soliciting feedback from your employee.

Identify New Goals, but Be Flexible

Now that you've assessed your employee's work against past goals, what new objectives should they be pursuing in the coming months? Many of your direct reports will have grown or developed over the course of the past year, mastering new skills and taking on new challenges. Think about updated goals in the context of previous conversations. Your employee's new targets should reflect any expanded abilities, development plans, and new departmental or organizational initiatives or priorities that have arisen since they last set goals.

Closing any performance gaps and tackling lingering issues should be the focus of your C players, but your solid and star contributors can have more leeway in setting their objectives, perhaps aligning them with developmental interests. As you did when you set goals in your previous performance-planning meeting, clearly define how the employee plans to reach their new objectives and set appropriate metrics for gauging success.

The beginning of a new cycle is also a good opportunity to establish or revise an employee's development plan. Determine what coaching, training, or other support will best equip them to reach their demanding new objectives and achieve even greater success in the next year.

While goals and development plans may have changed for your employee, keep your ongoing performance management processes in place. Continue your check-ins to assess progress toward goals, adjust plans, offer feedback and coaching, recognize good performance, and head off any burgeoning performance gaps.

Evaluate Your Approach

Effectively reviewing employees' performance takes practice, so use the transition time between cycles to evaluate your own performance as a manager during this process and consider how you might make improvements. Ask for feedback from your direct reports: How did the review process go? Were the feedback sessions effective? What was useful, and what wasn't? For instance, perhaps you didn't provide enough specific examples of performance gaps or give the person enough time to change based on your feedback before you followed up. Ask for suggestions for ways to do things differently in the future. You'll build trust when an individual sees you acting on the things they mention.

You can also evaluate yourself to assess your effectiveness. Consider the following questions, and take notes on your performance:

- Did you create an open climate for communication?

- Did you listen carefully to what the employee said? Did they feel heard?

- Was your feedback clear and specific? Was it useful and future focused?

- Did you spend enough time coaching?

- Were there times when you let bad performance slip, rather than giving immediate feedback?

- Did you focus sufficiently on employees' future development, or were you more focused on the present?

- What worked well, and what could be improved upon next time?

Compare your self-evaluation with any feedback from your direct reports, and determine what changes you can make in the future. Review your notes when preparing for performance reviews and periodically throughout the year as you prepare for ongoing development and check-in conversations.

Managing performance isn't easy, but with practice and thoughtful reflection you can become more comfortable with the process—and more effective in helping your employees succeed. But as with any process, there are always issues that need special attention. These obstacles are the focus of our final section.

Tough Topics

CHAPTER 16

Responding to the Steady Worker

Capable, solid employees rarely make waves. They get their jobs done well with little fanfare or oversight. They neither cause problems that require managerial intervention nor actively pursue the opportunity to take on more responsibility or expand their roles. In fact, these B players tend to make the fewest demands on your time, despite making up 80% of your workforce.

Because these employees may not be eager to advance in the organization or require immediate improvement, performance management for these solid B players can be confounding. Although they don't actively demand your attention, they still deserve your efforts to recognize and develop them. How can you best support your solid contributors and help them grow? It depends on what's driving them.

Who Are Your B Players?

B players tend to be reserved and averse to calling attention to themselves, even when they need to. "They are like the proverbial wheel that never squeaks—and, consequently, gets no grease," write Thomas J. DeLong and Vineeta Vijayaraghavan in their HBR article "Let's Hear It for B Players." Such reserve is alien to many A players, the lead singers and guitarists eager to solo, while B player drummers and bassists keep the band on beat. These steady contributors can work well on a team without feeling the need to stand out.

There are many reasons why these individuals choose to fly under the radar. Some B players are reformed A players who rejected the pressures of the "A" way of life. They place a high premium on work-life balance and are more interested in their day-to-day work than in their long-term careers. If they enjoy their work, they have no desire to be promoted from their roles. Others may have temporarily scaled back their ambitions to spend time with their young families or wish to devote time to meaningful pursuits and hobbies outside the workplace as they approach retirement age. Some solid performers are simply more risk averse and less entrepreneurial than their ambitious counterparts. Still others may be newly improved former C players.

B players tend to be loyal to organizations, shifting jobs less often and sticking around longer than A players. Responsible and service oriented, they bring increasing depth and stability to their work over time and accumulate valuable institutional memory. B players can quietly become go-to people thanks to their extensive organizational smarts. With strong networks and interpersonal connections, they know how to get things done.

Considering this expertise, these solid workers tend to be the backbone of many organizations. B players, like everyone else, need nurturing and recognition. Without encouragement, they can fall into the trap of seeing themselves as C players—or feel they're being taken for granted. Without some level of affirmation, they may lose their motivation and enthusiasm for their work.

No category is permanent, however. Your employee may be a solid worker at the moment, but in a year or two they could well be a rising star—or a struggling underperformer. It's important to make an explicit effort to acknowledge and foster their dedicated talent without pushing them in a direction they don't want to go. To retain them, you'll need to develop them in ways that best suit their competencies, potential, and desires.

Supporting Your Steady Workers

Managers don't always consider what they need to do to retain a good performer who demonstrates no interest in being promoted to management. Typically, management will ignore or overlook valuable B players until they get fed up and leave—or become C players.

While they may not want to stretch like their more ambitious peers, neither do they want to stagnate. To develop and motivate your solid contributors, begin the same way you would with your stars: Learn about their passions and interests, deepest work values, and strongest skills.

Understand B-player priorities, and offer growth

Psychological studies suggest we're tougher on people who differ from us than on those we identify with. Differences in ambition are a matter of temperament, a complex blend of motivation, personality, and intellect. Some managers are highly motivated, ambitious A players who may need to make a conscious effort not to undervalue B players who have different priorities. After all, some people produce solid work and prioritize getting home to family at the end of the day rather than focus on authority, influence, or power.

It's important to ask all your employees what they want from their careers, particularly when dealing with promising contributors you may feel tempted to push into new, more challenging positions. For some employees, lateral movements may be more attractive than upward promotion, and still others may not be interested in a change at all. Confirming what individuals really want out of their role in the organization can keep you from being disappointed if their ambitions don't match your plan for them. It's better to know the details of how they see their careers than to attempt to mentor an ambivalent protégé who, no matter what you do, won't be driven to pursue the same aspirations you hold dear. Some B players have reached the ceiling of their abilities, while others have made a conscious choice to stay in their current position.

Don't force an unwilling or uninterested B player to the A level, but do offer them opportunities to continue to learn, grow, and improve their skills. Stretch assignments, for example, can be invigorating opportunities to challenge your employees to acquire new skills, but choose such assignments carefully so you don't overwhelm them. Look for ways to make their jobs more interesting without burdening them with unwanted new responsibilities. Perhaps they'd appreciate training to bolster their strengths or the chance to attend a conference or seminar on a topic that excites them. Provide them with opportunities to grow within their comfort zone.

Your employee's priorities may change over time as well. If at first they tell you that they'd like to stay in their current role, check in periodically to find out if they've changed their mind, and if so, adjust their development plan accordingly.

Recognize and reward them

Strong and capable contributors can feel alienated or frustrated by a lack of attention, even if they don't seek out the spotlight. Track the frequency of your interactions with each of your direct reports. A players are rarely shy about asking for your time or stopping by to talk with you, but B players may be less likely to initiate contact. Make a point of regularly meeting with all of your employees, including the ones who never ask for it.

Acknowledge and praise B players' good work, and provide frequent affirmation. Recognition is especially important to workers who aren't gunning for a promotion. They neither expect nor receive the same financial rewards or promotions as A players, but they still crave acknowledgment of their very real contributions to the organization and want to feel appreciated and motivated. Tell them on a regular basis that they are valued, and tailor your praise to how each individual prefers to receive it. Some people appreciate public accolades, while others would prefer a simple handwritten note or a one-on-one conversation in which you thank them for their good work.

You can also show how much you trust and value your steady contributors by listening carefully to any ideas or suggestions they provide. Respond thoughtfully and respectfully. Show you recognize their contribution by giving them credit for any suggestions you act on, and demonstrate your trust by letting them be autonomous and make decisions appropriate for their skill level. You can also tap your capable contributors to mentor junior employees, demonstrating your trust in their knowledge and expertise.

All employees, not just stars, should be given opportunities for coaching, development, and—if they're interested—promotion, whether upward or lateral. Don't let your solid performers get lost in the crowd.

CHAPTER 17

Preventing Burnout on Your Team

Every once in a while, you'll encounter a poor performer who was once, according to your records, an excellent employee. This person is now just going through the motions and getting by—or worse, failing to meet expectations. What went wrong? You may be looking at a case of burnout.

Burnout is a debilitating state of work-related stress and a common danger for your best employees. People suffering from burnout will often exhibit three symptoms: exhaustion, cynicism, and inefficacy. Exhaustion includes physical, cognitive, and emotional fatigue so profound that it undermines a person's ability to work effectively and to feel good about what they're doing. Cynicism is an erosion of engagement—a way of distancing oneself psychologically from one's work. Inefficacy is a sense of incompetence and a lack of achievement and productivity.

This toxic cocktail manifests differently in each individual, but common signals include tiredness, lack of focus, expressions of anger or hopelessness, lower job performance and satisfaction, dwindling commitment to the organization, and a heightened desire to "do something different." Burnout can turn your A players into Bs and Bs into Cs. In some cases it's self-induced, but more often it's a result of heavy workloads, deadline pressures, and a nonstop workplace culture that precludes necessary rest and renewal.

As a manager, it's your job to ensure that your direct reports remain engaged and motivated in their work and performing at their highest capacity, which means helping them avoid taking on too much and encouraging them to take time to recharge.

Causes of Burnout

In a fast-paced, intense workplace where people are pressured to be perpetually on the clock, employees are more prone to anxiety, stress, and eventually burnout —especially top performers. Because it's not an official clinical term, hard data on the prevalence of burnout is elusive, but some researchers have found rates of burnout as high as 50% among medical residents and a whopping 85% among financial professionals.[1] In a 2015 Regus Group survey of more than 22,000 businesspeople across 100 countries, more than half (53%) reported being closer to burnout than they were just five years previously.[2]

Burnout occurs when an employee feels more stress than support in their work life. You risk burnout on your team if your employees are chronically overworked or under-rested. Common causes of burnout include:

- Work overload and extreme job demands, when people are given more work than can be reasonably accomplished in even a 60-hour workweek

- Streamlined staffing levels, when an individual is responsible for more work than one person can sustainably do

- The expectation of constant connectivity, when people feel pressured to work remotely (by email or phone) after work hours with little downtime

- The inability to avoid "low value-added" and monotonous tasks such as paperwork or unnecessary meetings

- Having too many projects to work on simultaneously, which creates interruptions and distractions and diminishes people's ability to focus and prioritize among projects

- High demands with low control, or conflicting demands—for example, "Think big and be creative, but don't make any mistakes"

Those most susceptible to burnout are your hardest-working, most-committed employees. They can become so involved in their jobs that they neglect other important parts of their lives, which can damage family and personal relationships as well as health. Managers can unwittingly contribute to employee burnout by relying too much on these individuals, loading all their critical projects on the same top performers—and then assigning them more important projects once they've succeeded. Don't make your employees choose between work and their mental and physical well-being. Even people who love their work shouldn't neglect everything else in their lives to take on more responsibilities.

Help Your Team Avoid Burnout

You can take steps to prevent burnout in your employees. Of course, occasional overwork may be unavoidable due to deadlines or peak work periods, but it shouldn't be constant. To keep your employees energized but not overworked, consider the following tactics.

Regularly monitor workloads, especially for your top performers

The very act of noticing an employee's overload can help them feel supported. Meet with each of your direct reports regularly to check in on how they're doing and to see if they are showing any indication that they may be overworked. (See the sidebar "Spot the Early Signs of Burnout.") If someone shows symptoms of burnout, look at their job description and their list of current tasks. It could be that they are juggling too many projects at once. Help them focus on doing one thing at a time by defining clear priorities for deliverables, ensuring that milestones don't overlap, and discerning the urgent from the important.

If the job's responsibilities are beyond the powers of even an exceptional worker, you may need to rethink their to-do list entirely. See if you can delegate some of the tasks to another team member (or even have a teammate step in temporarily to help), or consider redesigning the position.

Your employee may not want to admit to feeling overworked for fear that it will shed a negative light on them. But as a manager, you still need to see if they're able to handle everything on their plate. Get creative. For example, a major U.S. accounting firm monitored its employees' workloads by screening travel schedules. Individuals observed to be spending excessive time on the road or volunteering for too many projects were identified and counseled.

SPOT THE EARLY SIGNS OF BURNOUT

Burnout can be obvious in some people and more subtle in others. It will manifest differently in each individual. Here are some warning signs that your employee may be overworked:

- They struggle to concentrate or see the big picture.

- Routine or previously enjoyable tasks—even just getting to the office—appear difficult.

(continued)

SPOT THE EARLY SIGNS OF BURNOUT

- They seem disengaged or detached from their work, colleagues, and customers.

- They have grown increasingly negative, callous, or hostile.

- Their performance is slipping.

- They've expressed self-doubt or worry about completing tasks.

Your employee may not directly express their concern about their workload, so be a keen observer and an attentive listener. Acknowledge subtle cries for help: "I don't know how I'm going to keep up," "I'm swamped," or "It looks like I'll have to work over the weekend *again*."

If you spot any of these troubling signs, check in to gauge your employee's physical, cognitive, and emotional energy levels. If impending burnout is the problem rather than a personal issue or a temporary work upset, take corrective action before their performance suffers in the long term or they leave your company altogether.

Rein in excessive time demands

Many of us work in environments where we're expected to be accessible at all hours, even when we're on vacation. But constant connectivity costs us. Everyone needs rest and recovery time, and no one can sustain working all day, in the evening, and over the weekend. If people are available 24/7, they have no time to recharge.

With the exception of the occasional deadline, product launch, or emergency, don't require any employees to do more work than can be reasonably accomplished during a standard workweek ("standard" hours will vary across industries). Assess your team's current collective capacity, and ensure assignments and deadlines don't exceed it. Set boundaries: For example, demand that no emails are to be sent after 8 p.m. or on weekends.

Purposefully build in breaks

If you treat every day like a crisis and employees are chronically overworked, they won't have the energy, mental focus, resilience, or time to respond effectively if and when an actual crisis hits. Encourage your team to take breaks—from a simple lunch break to finally using their saved vacation time. Different fields have different busy times: Some must rush to meet end-of-year or end-of-quarter deadlines, some calendars orbit the do-or-die date of April 15, others are busiest when the school year kicks off. Identify a slow time when your employees can take a break—whether it's a short break during the day, an evening off during a crunch period, or a vacation. When individuals do take time off, build in enough teamwork and overlapping responsibilities to allow them to truly disconnect, without the need for employees to check their inbox for updates.

For example, professor Leslie Perlow and research associate Jessica Porter, both of Harvard Business School, worked with Boston Consulting Group (BCG) to see if it was possible to meet the high standards of service while still offering employees scheduled, uninterrupted time off. Each team assigned, in advance, at least one evening off per week for each team member to rest and recharge. They then adjusted the workload on the team so that others would cover for those individuals and their work wouldn't fall behind. The results were positive. According to Perlow and Porter, participants with rotating evenings off reported "higher job satisfaction, greater likelihood that they could imagine a long-term career at the firm, and higher satisfaction with work-life balance" than people on teams who didn't plan time off.[3] You can create a similar system that will let your team turn off and recharge on a regular basis, even if there's no natural break in your work cycle.

Allow for flexibility

It's not the number of hours worked but the quality of work that really matters. Instead of fretting about the time someone spends at their desk, help your employees design schedules that allow them to be more productive when they *are* working. Some folks work best in 90-minute periods followed by a 10-minute break, while others thrive on the "Pomodoro Technique" of 25-minute increments of work with 5-minute breaks. Create uninterrupted, meeting-free time for people to focus on important tasks that works with their rhythm and your needs.

Also consider the balance of priorities your employees have—not just in the office, but at home, too. People are at their most productive when they're able to adjust the time and place of their work to avoid conflicts with other responsibilities. If your top employee is struggling to get a full day of work in and arrive at home in time to deal with family demands, consider whether there are ways to allow them to get home earlier while still getting their best work from them. Your organization may have a formal program in place for you and your employees to take advantage of flextime or telecommuting arrangements, but if not, informal or ad hoc agreements can be just as or more effective. Work with your employees to design flexible arrangements that suit their job responsibilities, work styles, and personal demands.

Then, set them up for success. Advocate for the resources your people need to perform—by providing new technology or software, for example—to ensure your employees can work virtually without missing crucial communication or meetings.

Provide variety

People periodically need new challenges to stay motivated and committed, so vary your employees' tasks and responsibilities from time to time. Doing so will help your employees avoid burnout by shifting their attention to a fresh, exciting opportunity rather than feeling like they are in the same monotonous rut. You might, for example, give one person in your department responsibility for leading a team-based project for the next six months; after that time period, rotate the task to someone else. Instead of doling out responsibilities randomly, think about what might be the best options for each individual, and emphasize any professional-development benefits those opportunities might provide. Add these temporary responsibilities to the individual's performance objectives so that they're taken seriously.

While all of these steps can keep your employees from burning out, remember that they learn from you, their manager. If a direct reports sees you regularly eating at your desk, emailing late at night, or working through the weekend, they'll follow suit. Set an example, and follow these tips yourself. Not only will you show your employees it's OK to recharge, but you'll also avoid burnout yourself.

Being an attentive manager and deliberately watching for signs of burnout can help you keep your employees healthy and productive. Don't risk losing your top performers just because you're asking too much of them.

NOTES

1. "Statistics and Facts about Stress and Burnout," Statista.com, https://www.statista.com/topics/2099/stress-and-burnout.
2. Research by Regus Group, http://press.regus.com/hong-kong/majority-on-brink-of-stress.
3. Leslie A. Perlow and Jessica L. Porter, "Making Time Off Predictable—and Required," *Harvard Business Review*, October 2009 (product #R0910M).

CHAPTER 18

Managing the Performance of Remote Employees

Flexible work arrangements, telecommuting, and global offices may mean your employees aren't all sitting together in one central office. According to data from the Global Workplace Analytics, a research-based consulting organization, as of 2014, 3.7 million people worked remotely.[1] As virtual work arrangements become more common, you will likely need to apply the elements of performance management to someone you rarely, if ever, see in person.

Managing remote employees isn't fundamentally different than managing those who are physically present in your workplace, but communication challenges can easily arise when you're not colocated. Giving difficult feedback or discussing a tough performance review always requires special handling, but these tasks are further complicated when the person you're talking with isn't in the room with you to hear your tone or see subtle cues in body language. You'll need to put in extra effort to minimize the likelihood of off-site isolation, cultivate a positive team dynamic, address problems, and evaluate performance.

Whether your team members are in different time zones or simply working from home, you'll need to take a proactive approach to performance management.

Set Goals and Expectations

With remote employees, it's essential to establish a common purpose and to frame work in terms of individual team members' ambitions and needs. Clarify goals, and spell out specific guidelines for how you'll work together. Don't forget the details. Beyond identifying how projects will be divvied up, you may need to determine standards for communication that wouldn't be an issue with colocated employees, such as how the individual will collaborate with others on the team and how they'll communicate with you, their manager.

Just as you would with a direct report working in your office, schedule a performance-planning meeting, a one-on-one conversation to identify your remote employee's specific goals. Don't just trade emails; set up a video chat or, at a minimum, speak by phone. You'll have a more productive discussion, especially about professional aims and ambitions, when both of you can observe body language and hear tone and inflection. Carry the conversation much like you would with your other employees (as outlined in chapter 2), but make note of any challenges they may face because they aren't working regularly in your office. Consider if they will require additional resources to help them reach their objectives.

Once goals have been established, ask your employee to submit suggestions for meaningful performance metrics, especially for nonquantitative goals. Set clear targets—monthly, quarterly, and yearly performance milestones—to establish accountability. By collaborating with your employee in this way, they'll feel more invested in objectives, and they'll have a clear understanding about what they need to do to meet them. Finally, ensure that they know how they'll be evaluated—and assure them that you're using the same metrics you will use with the rest of your team, so they know that any future feedback or assessments will be fair.

Manage Performance and Communication

A key challenge for remote employees is isolation. Virtual workers are more prone to loneliness and loss of motivation, which can result in compromised performance. You probably won't get the opportunity to pick up visual cues or have impromptu conversations with a remote worker, so you'll need to make an extra effort to see how they're doing, keep an eye out for signs of burnout, and provide ongoing feedback. Keep the lines of communication open to prevent your remote employee from feeling truly isolated.

Just as with any other direct report, check in regularly on your remote employee's progress. You may need to be more rigorous about scheduling ongoing conversations with these workers than you would with team members you run into in the hallway or cafeteria. Even casual conversations with remote employees may need to be scheduled in advance.

When you touch base with your employee, choose communication tools carefully. Without physical cues, anyone can miss the subtleties of in-person interactions—especially during a tough conversation, such as when you're delivering constructive feedback. Face-to-face discussions are ideal, but don't hold off on having a crucial conversation or even a casual check-in just because you're waiting for an upcoming visit. Consider alternatives such as the phone, email, video, instant message, text, or group chat applications, but note that one platform won't work for every situation. Texting, IM, and team-messaging apps are lighter-touch options that carry lower emotional stakes. Information that might elicit an emotional response is better captured by phone or video, since they can allow you to project empathy, trust, concern, or firmness.

Phrase inquiries wisely when checking in. For example, when sending a quick email or IM, "Looking forward to seeing your product demo on Friday! Anything you need from me?" sounds enthusiastic and supportive. Compare this with something like "On track for Friday's deadline?" which may convey aggression and distrust.

Tracking performance from afar

When assessing work, tailor your approach to your remote employees. Take advantage of the opportunity to gather details about your direct reports' performance during team meetings. This may be the best time to assess how your remote employees work with their colleagues. Write each person's name on a pad of paper, and list their suggestions, questions, and comments. (If you find it too distracting to do this during the meeting, capture your observations immediately afterward.) When someone brings up a problem no one else has thought of, stubbornly repeats a point, or credits a colleague for doing good work, jot that down. Follow the same process as you observe conversations over discussion boards and group chats. Note who's giving helpful feedback, making smart suggestions, mediating conflict, or contributing in some other way. By capturing these details, you're creating a performance record you can refer to later.

As with any other employee, address performance issues with sensitivity. Start by gathering information. Your direct report's colleagues may have a different vantage point or more information on areas of concern. Keep in mind, though, that unless they're located in the same office as the remote worker, collaborators may not have a full picture either.

You can ask specific questions but also get more context with open-ended questions such as:

- "How's the project going with Ahkil overall?"

- "How are you finding him as a collaborator?"

- "Akhil has been doing a great job, but I'm wondering if I can do more to support his engagement. Have you observed anything that might help?"

- "You mentioned that Akhil has seemed checked out lately. When did that start? What do you think is going on?"

Handle these sensitive conversations with great care, and keep them confidential. The employee may not want a written record of any complaints or speculations, so hold these conversations by phone or video if you can't have them in person.

If you find that the situation warrants a discussion with your remote employee, prepare as you would for any feedback conversation. Consider the bigger picture: Do you know what else is going on in your employee's personal and professional life? Collect facts in advance, focus on observable behaviors, and don't speculate. Probe for root causes, so you feel fully prepared before having the conversation.

Giving feedback

When you notice something troubling in your remote employee's work that could grow into a performance gap if left unattended, address it with the same strategies you'd use in a traditional office setting. Follow up to investigate anomalies. You'll probably notice behavioral cues if someone is struggling or behind on their work. They might be uncharacteristically uncommunicative or have changed the frequency of their communications. They may seem frustrated, anxious, or even unusually relaxed before a major deadline while all their colleagues seem crunched. If you sense something is off, don't delay in reaching out to them.

When it comes to more-sensitive conversations—coaching, giving feedback, or discussing performance problems, for example—don't dictate the medium; ask your direct report what they prefer. You may well have a preference, perhaps for phone or video, but different tools can be more effective with different people. Video can provide helpful context and visual cues, but if the internet connection is poor it's more likely to be distracting than helpful. It may be worth investing in better technical gear, like a high-quality headset, to ensure you catch every nuance.

It can take special effort to give feedback effectively in a virtual setting. A written statement—say, "Your recent work contained some major problems"—seems much harsher than the same message delivered in conversation with a compassionate tone. Pay particular attention to timing. As with the employees you see regularly, you shouldn't plan to deliver tough criticism right before the person has another meeting or while they're in the last throes of a time-sensitive project. On the other hand, when it comes to recognizing strong performance, you don't need to be so careful. (Positive feedback, unlike criticism, can be delivered in writing, but your delivery will be more nuanced if you're communicating by phone or video.)

If you're using video when offering constructive feedback, position your camera at eye level; any lower will make it seem like you're looming above them. Maintain natural eye contact, and keep your body language open and relaxed. Start your conversation with the usual small talk, but make an extra effort to be warm. Because it can be difficult for people to pick up emotional cues by phone or video, be explicit about your positive feelings: "I really enjoy working with you. We've got some work to do, but I'm confident we'll get there." Express your appreciation for their work, or offer some positive feedback, if appropriate: what they are doing well or what they have made easier for you. Since your virtual employee may not have the opportunity to read your tone or body language, establishing this mutual trust and reassurance will help your message become more palatable. Keep in mind, though, that you don't want to couch your constructive comments in too much positivity, in case your request for improvement is lost. Just say enough to confirm to your employee that you're on the same team and on their side.

Limit your critical feedback to discussing a specific behavior. Offer concrete, narrowly focused comments that are free of speculation. Listen actively to their reply, and ask if anything seems wrong. If they won't meet your eyes in a video chat, for example, they could be feeling attacked, or it could just be due to camera placement.

End the conversation with an action item. Ideally, your direct report should offer a plan for fixing the problem themselves, at which point you can ask how you can help execute it. In some cases, though, you'll need to suggest a solution yourself. Thank them for the conversation before logging off, and follow up with an email summarizing how you agreed to proceed and reiterating your thanks.

Conduct the Appraisal Discussion

If your company requires a formal performance appraisal, that task can seem much harder when you're not seeing or talking to an employee on a regular basis. But if you've kept the lines of communication open throughout the review period, checked in with your employee, taken good notes, and provided feedback, you should have everything you need to help the process go smoothly.

Evaluate everyone equally

In traditional offices, it's easy to base assessments on observed face time: Who comes in early, stays late, and looks busy? But when a department allows employees to telecommute or is spread across multiple locations, management often develops a new process for evaluating remote individuals using specific metrics, while in-office workers are still assessed with the old approach. Face time unfairly becomes a factor in evaluating some but not others. While rarely a deliberate choice in the appraisal process, this disconnect in evaluation standards is especially problematic when an organization requires forced ranking. Remote employees may be "out of sight, out of mind" and overlooked for promotions or raises.

When employees work remotely, face time isn't something you can realistically assess and shouldn't be used as a performance metric. Instead, change your perspective to focus on the what and how of work. Evaluate the performance of remote employees in the same way as their office-based colleagues, and ensure that the same metrics are applied to everyone.

If you use a rating system, be sure to include context— concrete details that have contributed to the rating—in addition to a number. Remote workers are by nature somewhat isolated and may not have a good sense of how they and their colleagues are being evaluated. Receiving a numerical rating with no understanding of how it was decided does not make for a helpful or productive appraisal. Include details so the employee understands where they're falling short and how they can improve.

Avoid self-assessments

Unlike with your on-site employees, limit the use of self-assessments with your remote direct reports. Anyone who works alone much of the time can end up in a vacuum of their own perception. We all share the tendency to overrate our own abilities and take the credit for good results while denying our role in bad ones, but we're more likely to fall victim to these qualities when we're on our own. If your organization doesn't require self-assessments, don't use them. But if you must, emphasize to your virtual workers (as you would with the rest of your employees) that their self-evaluation is just one component of your performance review.

Conduct the conversation with care

Any employee can go through the motions of the appraisal process, never speaking their minds to avoid conflict—and the danger of this is greater with remote employees who may already feel disconnected. For a sensitive conversation like a performance review, ask your direct report how they'd be most comfortable meeting. Video conferencing will allow for a more-nuanced conversation, but if speaking by phone would make your employee more at ease, comply with their wishes. The more often you communicate by video during the course of the year, the more comfortable both of you will be using the medium, but if it's not something you do often, don't insist on it for an appraisal. Applying an unfamiliar technology to an already anxiety-inducing conversation may only make it more stressful for your employee. Accepting their preference will set a tone of participation and collaboration, increasing the likelihood that your remote direct report will feel comfortable being candid.

Tone of voice, facial expression, gestures, and non-verbal communication all matter in review conversations—particularly when you can't be together in person. Without contextual clues, misunderstandings can easily arise. As you did when giving feedback, be crystal clear when delivering feedback, and linger on positive messages. In the stress of an appraisal conversation, it's easy for anyone (particularly a remote worker) to focus more on constructive comments than on positive ones, so emphasize your positive feedback more than you might in an in-person meeting. After the discussion, continue the process again by setting up another meeting to establish goals and by keeping the lines of communication open.

Successfully managing your employees' performance involves a host of tasks and processes. Whether your employees are across the hall or across the globe, you should be ready to focus their efforts on the objectives that matter, work with them to move toward those goals, and ensure that they're growing, developing, and improving. Performance management may be changing rapidly, but by following the elements and best practices outlined in this guide, you can make managing performance a part of your regular routine and ensure that you get the best out of your people.

NOTE

1. GlobalWorkplaceAnalytics.com, "Latest Telecommuting Statistics," http://globalworkplaceanalytics.com/telecommuting-statistics.

Sources

General Sources

Buckingham, Marcus. "What Great Managers Do." *Harvard Business Review*, March 2005 (product #R0503D).

Buckingham, Marcus, and Ashley Goodall. "Reinventing Performance Management." *Harvard Business Review*, April 2015 (product #R1504B).

Cappelli, Peter, and Anna Tavis. "The Performance Management Revolution." *Harvard Business Review*, October 2016 (product #R1610D).

Dattner, Ben. "The Key to Performance Reviews Is Preparation." HBR.org, June 21, 2016 (product #H02WXG).

Ferrazzi, Keith. "7 Ways to Improve Employee Development Programs." HBR.org, July 31, 2015 (product #H028T9).

Goler, Lori, Janelle Gale, and Adam Grant. "Let's Not Kill Performance Evaluations Yet." *Harvard Business Review*, November 2016 (product #R1611G).

Grote, Dick. *How to Be Good at Performance Appraisals*. Boston: Harvard Business Review Press, 2011.

Harvard Business School Publishing. *Harvard Business Essentials: Performance Management*. Boston: Harvard Business School Press, 2006.

Harvard Business School Publishing. *HBR Guide to Coaching Employees*. Boston: Harvard Business Review Press, 2015.

Harvard Business School Publishing. *HBR Guide to Delivering Effective Feedback*. Boston: Harvard Business Review Press, 2016.

Harvard Business School Publishing. *Pocket Mentor: Developing Employees*. Boston: Harvard Business Press, 2009.

Harvard Business School Publishing. *Pocket Mentor: Setting Goals*. Boston: Harvard Business Press, 2009.

Harvard Business School Publishing. *20-Minute Manager: Performance Reviews*. Boston: Harvard Business Review Press, 2015.

Knight, Rebecca. "Delivering an Effective Performance Review." HBR.org, November 3, 2011. https://hbr.org/2011/11/delivering-an-effective-perfor.

Knight, Rebecca. "What to Do When Your Employee Asks for a Raise Too Soon." HBR.org, July 15, 2016 (product #H030GB).

McCord, Patty. "How Netflix Reinvented HR." *Harvard Business Review*, January–February 2014 (product #R1401E).

Wiseman, Liz. "An Easy Way to Make Your Employees Happier." HBR.org, November 13, 2014 (product #H01OZB).

Additional Chapter-by-Chapter Sources

Introduction
Cappelli, Peter. "The Annual Review Revolution." HBR.org Webinar, October 13, 2016. https://hbr.org/webinar/2016/09/the-annual-review-revolution.

Chapter 1
Grant, Heidi. "Nine Things Successful People Do Differently." *HBR Guide to Getting the Right Work Done*. Boston: Harvard Business Review Press, 2012.

Raynor, Michael E., and Derek Pankratz. "A Way to Know If Your Corporate Goals Are Too Aggressive." HBR.org, July 13, 2015 (product #H0278K).

Chapter 2
Bregman, Peter. "The Right Way to Hold People Accountable." HBR.org, January 11, 2016 (product #H02LQR).

Kirsner, Scott. "What Big Companies Get Wrong About Innovation Metrics." HBR.org, May 6, 2015 (product #H021XV).

Chapter 3
Grant, Heidi. "Get Your Team to Do What It Says It's Going to Do." *Harvard Business Review*, May 2014 (product #R1405E).

Chapter 4
Pozen, Robert C. "The Delicate Art of Giving Feedback." HBR.org, March 28, 2013. https://hbr.org/2013/03/the-delicate-art-of-giving-fee.

Zenger, Jack, and Joseph Folkman. "The Ideal Praise-to-Criticism
Ratio." HBR.org, March 15, 2013. https://hbr.org/2013/03/the
-ideal-praise-to-criticism.

Chapter 5
Gallo, Amy. "Giving a High Performer Productive Feedback." HBR.org,
December 3, 2009. https://hbr.org/2009/12/giving-a-high
-performer-produc.
Grant, Heidi. "Sometimes Negative Feedback Is Best." HBR.org, January
28, 2013. https://hbr.org/2013/01/sometimes-negative-feedback-is.
Grenny, Joseph. "How to Make Feedback Feel Normal." HBR.org,
August 19, 2016 (product #H032G0).

Chapter 6
Hill, Linda, and Kent Lineback. "To Build Trust, Competence Is Key."
HBR.org, March 22, 2012. https://hbr.org/2012/03/to-build
-trust-competence-is-k.
Valcour, Monique. "You Can't Be a Great Manager If You're Not a
Good Coach." HBR.org, July 17, 2014 (product #H00WOP).

Chapter 7
Cable, Dan, and Freek Vermeulen. "Stop Paying Executives for Perfor-
mance." HBR.org, February 23, 2016 (product #H02OEX).
Harvard Business School Publishing. "Employee Recognition and
Reward When Times Are Tough." *Harvard Management Update.*
September 2003. https://hbr.org/2008/02/employee-recognition-
and-rewar-1.html.
Hope, Jeremy, and Steve Player. *Beyond Performance Management.*
Boston: Harvard Business Review Press, 2012.
Kohn, Alfie. "Why Incentive Plans Cannot Work." *Harvard Business
Review*, September–October 1993 (product #93506).
Novak, David. "Recognizing Employees Is the Simplest Way to
Improve Morale." HBR.org, May 9, 2016 (product #H02VEN).
Porath, Christine. "Half of Employees Don't Feel Respected by Their
Bosses." HBR.org, November 19, 2014 (product #H012OO).
Porath, Christine, and Christine Pearson. "The Price of Incivility." *Har-
vard Business Review*, January–February 2013 (product #R1301J).
Spreitzer, Gretchen, and Christine Porath. "Creating Sustainable
Performance." *Harvard Business Review*, January–February 2012
(product #R1201F).
Valcour, Monique. "The Power of Dignity in the Workplace." HBR.org,
April 28, 2014 (product #H00S6P).

Chapter 8

Andersen, Erika. "How to Decide What Skill to Work On Next." HBR.org, January 25, 2016 (product #H02M5W).

Butler, Timothy, and James Waldroop. "Job Sculpting: The Art of Retaining Your Best People." *Harvard Business Review*, September–October 1999 (product #99502).

Donovan, John, and Cathy Benko. "AT&T's Talent Overhaul." *Harvard Business Review*, October 2016 (product #R1610E).

Gino, Francesca, and Bradley Staats. "Developing Employees Who Think for Themselves." HBR.org, June 3, 2015 (product #H0248M).

Herzberg, Frederick. "One More Time: How Do You Motivate Employees?" *Harvard Business Review*, January 2003 (product #R0301F).

Jen Su, Amy. "The Questions Good Coaches Ask." HBR.org, December 12, 2014 (product #H01R6J).

Valcour, Monique. "If You're Not Helping People Develop, You're Not Management Material." HBR.org, January 23, 2014 (product #H00MXT).

Chapter 9

Gallo, Amy. "Demystifying Mentoring." HBR.org, February 1, 2011 (product #H006S6).

Harvard Business School Publishing. *HBR Guide to Getting the Mentoring You Need.* Boston: Harvard Business Review Press, 2014.

Hewlett, Sylvia Ann. "The Real Benefit of Finding a Sponsor." HBR.org, January 26, 2011. https://hbr.org/2011/01/the-real-benefit-of-finding-a.

Hewlett, Sylvia Ann. "The Right Way to Find a Career Sponsor." HBR.org, September 11, 2013. https://hbr.org/2013/09/the-right-way-to-find-a-career-sponsor.

Hoffman, Reid, Ben Casnocha, and Chris Yeh. "Tours of Duty: The New Employer-Employee Compact." *Harvard Business Review*, June 2013 (product #R1306B).

Tjan, Anthony K. "Keeping Great People with Three Kinds of Mentors." HBR.org, August 12, 2011 (product #H007LK).

Chapter 10

Brendel, David. "Asking Open-Ended Questions Helps New Managers Build Trust." HBR.org, September 17, 2015 (product #H02CEG).

Goldsmith, Marshall. "Empowering Your Employees to Empower Themselves." HBR.org, April 23, 2010. https://hbr.org/2010/04/empowering-your-employees-to-e.

Petriglieri, Gianpiero. "Learning Is the Most Celebrated Neglected Activity in the Workplace." HBR.org, November 6, 2014 (product #HO12ON).

Wiseman, Liz, and Greg McKeown. "Bringing Out the Best in Your People." *Harvard Business Review*, May 2010 (product #R1005K).

Chapter 11

Baldoni, John. "The Three Cs of Dealing with Under Performers." HBR.org, September 10, 2008. https://hbr.org/2008/09/underperformers.

Gallo, Amy. "Help! I'm an Underperformer." HBR.org, October 5, 2010. https://hbr.org/2010/10/help-im-an-underperformer.

Gallo, Amy. "How to Help an Underperformer." HBR.org, June 23, 2014 (product #HOOVK2).

Gallo, Amy. "Making Sure Your Employees Succeed." HBR.org, February 7, 2011. https://hbr.org/2011/02/making-sure-your-employees-suc.

Hill, Linda, and Kent Lineback. "The Most Important Question a Manager Can Ask." HBR.org, April 18, 2011. https://hbr.org/2011/04/the-most-important-question-a.

Maignan Wilkins, Muriel. "Is Your Employee Coachable?" HBR.org, February 19, 2015 (product #HO1VYV).

Chapter 12

Baldassarre, Leonardo, and Brian Finken. "GE's Real-Time Performance Development." HBR.org, August 12, 2015 (product #HO29L8).

Buckingham, Marcus. "What If Performance Management Focused on Strengths?" HBR.org, December 3, 2013. https://hbr.org/2013/12/what-if-performance-management-focused-on-strengths.

Cappelli, Peter. "The Common Myths About Performance Reviews, Debunked." HBR.org, July 26, 2016 (product #HO30NZ).

Grote, Dick. "Every Manager Needs to Practice Two Types of Coaching." HBR.org, September 30, 2016 (product #HO35HV).

Rock, David. "Give Your Performance Management System a Review." HBR.org, June 14, 2013. https://hbr.org/2013/06/give-your-performance-manageme.

Chapter 13

Dattner, Ben. "In Performance Appraisals, Make Context Count."
HBR.org, June 3, 2013. https://hbr.org/2013/06/in-performance
-appraisals-make.

Grote, Dick. "Performance Appraisal Reappraised." *Harvard Business
Review*, January–February 2000 (product #F00105).

Harvard Business School Publishing. *HBR Guide to Delivering Effective Feedback Ebook + Tools*. Boston: Harvard Business Review
Press, 2016.

Chapter 16

DeLong, Thomas J., and Vineeta Vijayaraghavan. "Let's Hear It
for B Players." *Harvard Business Review*, June 2003 (product
#R0306F).

Chapter 17

Behson, Scott. "Don't Treat Your Career Marathon Like a Sprint."
HBR.org, October 11, 2013. https://hbr.org/2013/10/dont-treat
-your-career-marathon-like-a-sprint.

Behson, Scott. "Just Because You're Happy Doesn't Mean You're Not
Burned Out." HBR.org, July 13, 2015 (product #H027AF).

Fernandez, Rich. "Help Your Team Manage Stress, Anxiety, and Burnout." HBR.org, January 21, 2016 (product #H02M4Z).

Perlow, Leslie A., and Jessica L. Porter. "Making Time Off Predictable—and Required." *Harvard Business Review*, October 2009
(product #R0910M).

Schwartz, Tony. "Take Back Your Attention." HBR.org, February 9,
2011. https://hbr.org/2011/02/take-back-your-attention.

Valcour, Monique. "Beating Burnout." *Harvard Business Review*,
November 2016 (product #R1611H).

Wilson, H. James. "The Surprising Power of Impulse Control."
HBR.org, February 25, 2014 (product #H00OSS).

Chapter 18

Batista, Ed. "Tips for Coaching Someone Remotely." HBR.org,
March 18, 2015 (product #H01XI4).

Ferrazzi, Keith. "Evaluating the Employees You Can't See." HBR.
org, December 20, 2012. https://hbr.org/2012/12/evaluating
-the-employees-you-c.

Ferrazzi, Keith. "Getting Virtual Teams Right," *Harvard Business
Review*, December 2014 (product #R1412J).

Graber, Sean. "Why Remote Work Thrives in Some Companies and Fails in Others." HBR.org, March 20, 2015 (product #H01Y22).

Harvard Business School Publishing. *20-Minute Manager: Leading Virtual Teams*. Boston: Harvard Business Review Press, 2016.

Harvard Business School Publishing. *20-Minute Manager: Virtual Collaboration*. Boston: Harvard Business Review Press, 2016.

Knight, Rebecca. "How to Manage Remote Direct Reports." HBR.org, February 10, 2015 (product #H01VI9).

Rayess, Randy. "5 Basic Needs of Virtual Workforces." HBR.org, March 17, 2015 (product #H01X2Z).

Index

**Harvard
Business
Review**

Invaluable insights
always at your fingertips

With an All-Access subscription to
Harvard Business Review, you'll get
so much more than a magazine.

Exclusive online content and tools
you can put to use today

My Library, your personal workspace for sharing,
saving, and organizing HBR.org articles and tools

Unlimited access to more than 4,000 articles in the
Harvard Business Review archive

Subscribe today at hbr.org/subnow

Smart advice and inspiration from a source you trust.

If you enjoyed this book and want more comprehensive guidance on essential professional skills, turn to the HBR Guides Boxed Set. Packed with the practical advice you need to succeed, this seven-volume collection provides smart answers to your most pressing work challenges, from writing more effective emails and delivering persuasive presentations to setting priorities and managing up and across.

Harvard Business Review Guides

Available in paperback or ebook format. Plus, find downloadable tools and templates to help you get started.

- Better Business Writing
- Building Your Business Case
- Buying a Small Business
- Coaching Employees
- Delivering Effective Feedback
- Finance Basics for Managers
- Getting the Mentoring You Need
- Getting the Right Work Done
- Leading Teams
- Making Every Meeting Matter
- Managing Stress at Work
- Managing Up and Across
- Negotiating
- Office Politics
- Persuasive Presentations
- Project Management

HBR.ORG/GUIDES

Buy for your team, clients, or event.
Visit hbr.org/bulksales for quantity discount rates.

Harvard
Business
Review
Press

CPSIA information can be obtained
at www.ICGtesting.com
Printed in the USA
LVHW091952300619
622764LV00012BB/273/P